# LISTS TO LIVE BY

LISTS TO LIVE BY
published by Multnomah Publishers, Inc.

Copyright © 1999 by Alice Gray, Steve Stephens, John Van Diest

*International Standard Book Number: 1-57673-478-1*
Printed in the United States of America

Cover and interior design by Stephen Gardner

The lists in this book are not substitutes for obtaining professional advice
from qualified persons and organizations. Consult the appropriate
professional advisor for complete and updated information.

Every effort has been made to provide proper and accurate source attributions for
selections in this volume. If any attribution is incorrect, the publisher welcomes written
documentation supporting correction for subsequent printings. The publisher gratefully
acknowledges the cooperation of publishers and individuals granting permission
for use of selections. Please see the acknowledgements for full attribution of these sources.

Scripture quotations are from the following translations:

The Holy Bible, New International Version (NIV) © 1973, 1984
by International Bible Society, used by permission of Zondervan Publishing House

The Holy Bible, King James Version (KJV)

The New Testament in Modern English, Revised Edition (Phillips)
1958, 1960, 1972 by J. B. Phillips

Holy Bible, New Living Translation (NLT) © 1996.
Used by permission of Tyndale House Publishers, Inc. All rights reserved.

The Message
© 1993 by Eugene H. Peterson

For information:
MULTNOMAH PUBLISHERS, INC.
P.O. BOX 1720
SISTERS, OR 97759

**Congress Cataloging-in-Publication Data:**
List to live by: for everything that really matters/compiled by Alice Gray, Steve Stephens,
and John Van Diest. p.cm. Includes bibliographical references. ISBN 1 57673 478 1 (alk. paper)
1. Conduct of life. I. Gray, Alice, 1939– II. Stephens, Steve. III. Van Diest, John.
BJ1581.2.L55   1999   99-12863   646.7–dc21   CIP

00   01   02   03   04   05   06  —  10  9  8  7  6  5   4   3

# LISTS
## to live by

*For everything that really matters.*

COMPILED BY
ALICE GRAY, STEVE STEPHENS, AND JOHN VAN DIEST

Multnomah® Publishers *Sisters, Oregon*

# CONTENTS

# FOR EVERYTHING THAT REALLY MATTERS

*You name it and this book has it—well, almost!*
*It's more than trivia—it is life changing.*
*It's more than opinions—it is timeless truth.*
*It's more than words—it is motivating.*
*It's more than a collection—it is a treasure.*

Lists are a great way of wrapping up powerful thoughts in an easy and accessible package. You can read them one at a time, pondering and reflecting on each point. Or you can read them in bunches. Start at the beginning and work your way through to the treasures at the end, or jump around to your favorites. Read them when you're on the run, or curl up with a steaming cup of hot chocolate.

Within these pages are dynamic ideas covering a gamut of topics from contentment to friendship, from family to virtue. The lists are brief and usable, and at the same time, valuable and thought provoking. However you approach it, Lists to Live By is so full of good concepts and ideas that you will likely come back to it over and over again. And you'll find yourself sharing the practical wisdom in conversation with your business associates, family, and friends.

We have carefully selected two hundred lists which we hope will impact you in such a way that your life will be easier and richer and truer. Some will cause you to reflect. Some will bring excitement. Some will make you smile. Some will move you to action. Some might even change your life.

ALICE GRAY    DR. STEVE STEPHENS    JOHN VAN DIEST

# SUCCESS
*Growing through learning and creativity*

1

# THREE SECRETS TO SUCCESS

1.

*Be willing to learn new things.*

2.

*Be able to assimilate new information quickly.*

3.

*Be able to get along with and work with other people.*

SALLY RIDE
ASTRONAUT

# FIVE REASONS IT'S EASIER TO SUCCEED

### 1.
*It's easier to succeed because failure exacts a high price
in terms of time when you have to do a job over.*

### 2.
*It's easier to succeed because success
eliminates the agony and frustration of defeat.*

### 3.
*It's easier to succeed because money spent to fail
must be spent again to succeed.*

### 4.
*It's easier to succeed because a person's
credibility decreases with each failure, making it
harder to succeed the second time.*

### 5.
*And it's easier to succeed because joy and expressions of
affirmation come from succeeding, whereas feelings
of discouragement and discontent accompany failure.*

CATHY S. TRUETT, FOUNDER, CHICK-FIL-A COMPANY
FROM "IT'S EASIER TO SUCCEED THAN TO FAIL"

# SIX WAYS TO BURY A GOOD IDEA

### 1.

*It will never work.*

### 2.

*We've never done it that way before.*

### 3.

*We're doing fine without it.*

### 4.

*We can't afford it.*

### 5.

*We're not ready for it.*

### 6.

*It's not our responsibility.*

AUTHOR UNKNOWN
AS CITED IN "MORE OF...THE BEST OF BITS & PIECES," ROB GILBERT, PH.D., ED.

# TAKING CONTROL OF YOUR TIME

### 1.

Remember who's in charge. Time is something you manage, not something that manages you. Learn to think through each time commitment in its entirety. Buy yourself time to think by asking, "Can I let you know tomorrow?"

### 2.

Decide what is truly urgent. Rather than think, "I must get this done now!" Try putting it off. Surprise! Most "urgent" needs aren't really that urgent.

### 3.

Schedule in reverse. Put the *real* priorities on the calendar first—family picnic or date night. Then write in everything else.

### 4.

Drop one thing from your schedule. You'll probably let someone down, but look who benefits. Spending two less days a month as a lunch monitor at your son's school frees you up for a lunch date with your spouse.

## 5.

Be, rather than do. Try it for an evening. Think. Pray. Relax in a lawn chair.

## 6.

Get your spouse's perspective. Ask your mate to comment on how you're using your time and what seems to be robbing you of time.

## 7.

Be honest about your limitations. Do you find yourself saying "yes" to a project in the hopes that a weekend will suddenly hold the ten extra hours you'd need to complete it? You can't manufacture time.

## 8.

Make a list of your commitments. Post the list next to the phone or your calendar. A visual reminder of all that you're involved with will make you think twice before tacking on something else.

LOUISE A. FERREBEE, ASSOCIATE EDITOR
FROM "MARRIAGE PARTNERSHIP" MAGAZINE

# 25 TRAITS OF ENTREPRENEURS

| | |
|---:|:---|
| DRIVE | *a high degree of motivation* |
| COURAGE | *tenacity and persistence* |
| GOALS | *a sense of direction* |
| KNOWLEDGE | *and a thirst for it* |
| GOOD HEALTH | *taking care of one's body* |
| HONESTY | *especially intellectual* |
| OPTIMISM | *positive attitude* |
| JUDGMENT | *knowing the wise from the foolish* |
| ENTHUSIASM | *excitement about life* |
| CHANCE TAKING | *willingness to risk failure* |
| DYNAMISM | *energy* |
| ENTERPRISE | *willingness to tackle tough jobs* |
| PERSUASION | *ability to sell* |
| OUTGOINGNESS | *friendly* |

| | |
|---|---|
| PATIENT YET IMPATIENT | *patient with others, yet* |
| | *impatient with the status quo* |
| ADAPTABILITY | *capable of change* |
| PERFECTIONISM | *desire to achieve excellence* |
| HUMOR | *ability to laugh at self and others* |
| VERSATILITY | *broad interests and skills* |
| CURIOSITY | *interested in people and things* |
| SELF-IDENTITY | *self-esteem and self-sufficiency* |
| REALISM/IDEALISM | *occupied by reality* |
| | *but guided by ideals* |
| IMAGINATION | *seeking new ideas, combinations,* |
| | *and relationships* |
| COMMUNICATION | *articulate* |
| RECEPTIVE | *alert* |

EARL NIGHTINGALE
CO-FOUNDER OF NIGHTINGALE AND CONANT CORPORATION

SUCCESS

# HOW TO GIVE
# CONSTRUCTIVE CRITICISM

### 1.
#### CONSIDER YOUR MOTIVE FIRST.

*What do you desire to accomplish? Is it selfish?
Is it from anger or hurt feelings? Will what you say benefit others?*

### 2.
#### WRITE DOWN WHAT YOU WILL SAY.

*Begin with any affirmations that are sincere about the other person.
Use facts, opinions, intuitions, and feelings.
Read it over several times and rewrite until it sounds like what you
want to convey. Practice saying it out loud in front of a mirror.*

### 3.
#### ASK FOR AN APPOINTMENT TO SPEAK
#### WITH THE OTHER PERSON.

*Be amiable to his or her schedule. Say, "I have something I have
been thinking about, and I want to share it with you."*

### 4.
#### SET ASIDE ALL EXPECTATIONS AND ACCUSATIONS.

*Be open to hearing the other's reasoning. Don't argue.
Knowing your motives as suggested above will
help you communicate without arguing.*

### 5.
#### THANK THE OTHER PERSON FOR LISTENING.

GLENDA HOTTON
MARRIAGE AND FAMILY THERAPIST

# WHY WE PROCRASTINATE

We feel overwhelmed.

We overestimate the amount of time needed.

We would rather be doing something else.

We think that if we wait long enough, the task will go away.

We fear failure.

We fear success.

We enjoy the last-minute adrenaline rush.

BOB AND EMILIE BARNES
FROM "THE 15-MINUTE MONEY MANAGER"

# EIGHT THINGS YOU NEED
# TO KNOW ABOUT FAILURE

1.

## TO FAIL IS NOT THE SAME AS BEING A FAILURE.

*One may have many failings and yet still be far from being a failure.*

2.

## TO FAIL IS NOT THE DISGRACE EVERYONE THINKS IT IS.

*To err is to do nothing more than to join the human race.*

3.

## FAILURE IS ONLY A TEMPORARY SETBACK.

*Failure is never the final chapter of the book of your life
unless you give up and quit.*

4.

## NOTHING WORTHWHILE IS EVER ACHIEVED
## WITHOUT RUNNING THE RISK OF FAILURE.

*The man who risks everything to try to achieve something truly
worthwhile and fails is anything but a disgraceful failure.*

### 5.
### FAILURE IS A NATURAL PREPARATION FOR SUCCESS.

*Strange as it may seem to some of you, success*
*is much more difficult to live with successfully than is failure.*

### 6.
### EVERY FAILING BRINGS WITH IT THE POSSIBILITIES OF
### SOMETHING GREATER.

*Analyze failure under whatever circumstances you choose, and you will*
*discover some seeds for turning failure into success.*

### 7.
### WHAT YOU DO WITH FAILURES IN YOUR LIFE IS UP TO YOU.

*Failure is either a blessing or a curse, depending upon the*
*individual's reaction or response to it.*

### 8.
### FAILINGS ARE OPPORTUNITIES TO LEARN HOW TO
### DO THINGS BETTER THE NEXT TIME—
### TO LEARN WHERE THE PITFALLS ARE AND HOW TO AVOID THEM.

*The best possible thing to do with failure is to learn all you can from it.*

DALE GALLOWAY, DEAN, SCHOOL OF CHURCH LEADERSHIP AND BIBLICAL PREACHING,
ASBURY THEOLOGICAL SEMINARY, WILMORE, KY, FROM "HOW TO FEEL LIKE A SOMEBODY AGAIN!"

# COMMONLY ASKED
# INTERVIEW QUESTIONS

### 1.
### TELL ME ABOUT YOURSELF.

*Keep your answer brief. He or she is interested in your goals, experience, interests, and communication skills.*

### 2.
### WHAT ARE YOUR STRENGTHS/WEAKNESSES?

*Emphasize your good traits and those that relate to the job for which you are interviewing. You can mention an area that you're working to improve or one in which you have recently made great strides.*

### 3.
### WHY DO YOU WANT TO WORK HERE?

*This is a good chance to mention how you can apply your skills, interests, and goals to the job.*

### 4.
### WHY SHOULD WE HIRE YOU?

*Take this opportunity to highlight the unique qualities you can bring to the job.*

### 5.
### WHAT WOULD YOU DO IN (A PARTICULAR SITUATION)?

*Don't be afraid to say that you would ask questions of your supervisor and approach each challenge as a learning opportunity.*

SELECTED FROM "ABOUT...GETTING YOUR FIRST JOB" A "LIFE ADVICE®" PAMPHLET
PUBLISHED BY METLIFE'S CONSUMER EDUCATION CENTER

# WHAT TO INCLUDE ON A RESUME

### A HEADER

Located at the top, this should include your name, address, and phone number.

### EDUCATION

List the most recent diploma or degree you have earned or are working toward, the date of graduation, and your field of study.

### WORK EXPERIENCE

List employers, job titles, the dates worked, and a brief description of your duties, starting with the most recent. You may also want to include volunteer work or part-time jobs.

### SKILLS

This is optional. List computer and language skills or other skills that may be relevant to the job for which you are applying.

### HONORS AND ACTIVITIES

List awards you have earned, clubs or organizations to which you belong, and activities in which you participate.

### REFERENCES

Include the notation, "References will be provided upon request." You should be prepared to provide the names of at least three people who can attest to your ability and personality. (Be sure to tell your references ahead of time that you may be using them, so they are not caught off guard when an employer calls to ask about you.)

SELECTED FROM "ABOUT...GETTING YOUR FIRST JOB," A "LIFE ADVICE®" PAMPHLET
PUBLISHED BY METLIFE'S CONSUMER EDUCATION CENTER

# TOP 10 LIST FOR INTERVIEWEES

### 1.
#### COME PREPARED.

Do research in advance about the company. Interviewees who do their homework find themselves more confident and better prepared to answer questions about the responsibilities of a current open position.

### 2.
#### BRING A CLEAN COPY OF AN UP-TO-DATE RESUME.

Resumes should list major accomplishments and results achieved. Resumes should be no more than two pages. Bring a separate folder to the interview containing examples of your work, reference letters, etc.

### 3.
#### DRESS THE PART.

At least one day prior to your interview, examine the outfit you plan to wear to the interview (including shoes). Leave strong perfume and cologne at home. It's better to be conservative than flashy during interviews.

### 4.
#### PLAN TO ARRIVE TEN MINUTES EARLY.

Make sure you know how to get where you are going and allow for enough time to collect your thoughts before your appointment.

### 5.
#### KNOW WHY YOU WANT THE JOB.

Be prepared to answer the questions, whether asked directly or indirectly, why you want this particular job and why you would be the best choice for it.

### 6.
#### LISTEN TO YOUR INTERVIEWER'S QUESTIONS CAREFULLY.

Be prepared to answer difficult questions under pressure. If you need an extra few seconds to prepare your answer, it is okay to ask the interviewer to repeat and/or clarify the question.

## 7.
### ANSWER WITH ENTHUSIASM AND PROFESSIONAL VOCABULARY.

Avoid slang. Highlight appropriate aspects of your education, work experience, and continuing education (seminars, training, etc.). Convey enthusiasm. Body language is important. Make eye contact with your interviewer.

## 8.
### BE PREPARED TO DISCUSS AREAS YOU NEED TO STRENGTHEN IN YOUR WORK EXPERIENCE AND KNOWLEDGE.

It's hard to trust an interviewee who expresses no limitations in his or her performance. Avoid trying to present a perfect image.

## 9.
### BRING QUESTIONS OF YOUR OWN.

The interviewee who asks informed questions about the company and the position is set apart from the crowd. Don't be afraid to ask information about what the company has to offer you.

## 10.
### FOLLOW UP AFTER THE INTERVIEW WITH A THANK-YOU.

Within twenty-four hours, send a postcard or brief letter thanking the interviewer for the opportunity to interview for the job. Include something specific that was discussed during your time together. Call five to ten days later and let the interviewer know you are still interested in the job.

LANI WILLIAMS
DIRECTOR OF ADVANCEMENT, WESTERN SEMINARY

# 10 QUALITIES OF SUCCESSFUL BOSSES

### 1.
Cheerfully greets all employees with a
smile regardless of their job status.

### 2.
Properly calls people by name
(and title when appropriate).

### 3.
Never considers himself or herself "above" doing
menial tasks or helping someone.

### 4.
Delegates but does not dump his or her tasks on others.

### 5.
Privately and constructively critiques an employee who
has made an error, no matter how insignificant or egregious.

### 6.
Displays an appropriate sense of humor
in the proper circumstances.

### 7.
Is self-deprecating, always willing to take responsibility
for errors, never placing blame on others.

### 8.
Is not self-absorbed, but interested in
others—an attentive listener.

### 9.
Never expects employees to keep rules
he or she is unwilling to observe.

### 10.
Treats employees of the opposite sex as business
professionals and does not require females to do
the traditionally "old-fashioned female chores."

JUNE HINES MOORE, MOORE THAN MANNERS CONSULTING
FROM "THE ETIQUETTE ADVANTAGE"

# 12 QUALITIES OF SUCCESSFUL EMPLOYEES

## 1.
Always introduce people in a manner that
makes the two of them comfortable.

## 2.
Always write a note or letter to acknowledge a gift or favor.

## 3.
Be able to converse intelligently on a variety
of subjects. Don't pretend to be a "know-it-all"
on any topic of conversation. Don't brag.

## 4.
Know how to dress properly on and off the
job and in keeping with the company image.

## 5.
Never discuss private company matters with outsiders.

## 6.
Maintain the appearance of dignity but not superiority.

**7.**
Keep promises, obligations, and appointments. Always
be on time. If detained, notify the host or guest.

**8.**
Return telephone calls within twenty-four hours
or ask assistance in doing so.

**9.**
Don't procrastinate or neglect your duties and conse
quently burden someone else's schedule.

**10.**
Return "borrowed" property quickly and in good condition.

**11.**
Don't engage in office gossip, but attempt to stop rumors.

**12.**
Give recognition, and don't take credit for someone else's work.

JUNE HINES MOORE, MOORE THAN MANNERS CONSULTING
FROM "THE ETIQUETTE ADVANTAGE"

# 14 WAYS TO SHOCK YOUR BOSS

### 1.
Show up to work early.

### 2.
Take the initiative to ask questions.

### 3.
Ask for advice, use it, then thank your boss.

### 4.
Speak well of your boss behind his or her back.

### 5.
When necessary, willingly stay late to finish an important project.

### 6.
Do more than your share of work.

### 7.
Be willing to work odd shifts.

### 8.
Every morning, come prepared to work hard.

**9.**
Continue to grow professionally.

**10.**
Read whatever you can about your field.

**11.**
Suggest new ideas that will save the company time and money.

**12.**
Stick around—don't always look for greener pastures.

**13.**
Pray for your boss.

**14.**
Invite your boss to church.

DAVID SANFORD, SENIOR DIRECTOR OF PUBLISHING,
LUIS PALAU EVANGELISTIC ASSOCIATION

# 12 STEPS TO CREATIVE THINKING

### 1.
#### RIGHT AWAY, WRITE IT DOWN.
*Record ideas as soon as you think of them. Keep paper and pen handy at all times—in your car, by your television, on your nightstand.*

### 2.
#### LISTEN TO MUSIC.
*Listen to whatever sparks your imagination, whether it's Bach, the Beatles, or something you've never heard before.*

### 3.
#### EXERCISE.
*Go for a run, shoot some hoops, do jumping jacks—anything that starts your blood pumping and keeps your mind sharp.*

### 4.
#### BRAINSTORM WITH A FRIEND, CO-WORKER, OR SIX-YEAR-OLD.
*Talk with someone who looks at the world a little differently than you do. Chances are he or she will inspire a new approach.*

### 5.
#### DO IT POORLY.
*If you're a perfectionist, don't be. Create something that isn't necessarily your best work, but that gets the job done. Then go back later to fix it or redo it.*

### 6.
#### WATCH PEOPLE.
*Go downtown or to the mall, sit on a bench, and observe the passersby. Imagine what kind of life they lead.*

## 7.
### KEEP A JOURNAL.

*Write about your life and what's important to you, then
revisit your old thoughts when you need new ideas.*

## 8.
### PRAY OR READ THE BIBLE.

*Putting life into spiritual perspective can take the
pressure off and jump-start the creative juices.*

## 9.
### FREE-WRITE.

*Sit down at the computer or with pen and paper and write whatever
comes into your mind. You might be surprised at what comes out.*

## 10.
### CHANGE YOUR LOCALE.

*Find a new quiet place—a park, the beach, a library, or
just a different room—and let your mind wander.*

## 11.
### WASH THE DISHES OR MOW THE LAWN.

*It's easy and it gives you a feeling of
accomplishment while you're trying to think.*

## 12.
### SLEEP ON IT.

*If nothing is working, your best bet may be to give up for now. Let your
subconscious create overnight and you'll have fresh ideas tomorrow.*

JAMES LUND
MARKETING COPY EDITOR

# HOW TO BECOME
# A LIFELONG LEARNER

## 1.
### START WITH YOUR ATTITUDE.

Lifelong learning begins with a heart that desires change, wisdom, and application.

## 2.
### ASK QUESTIONS.

Learners ask good questions. They possess an insatiable curiosity— a longing to know, discover, inquire. Ask questions that get below the surface.

## 3.
### JOIN OTHERS.

Collaborative learning—in classes, small groups, with friends and colleagues—allows us to benefit from diverse perspectives and approaches. People are a gold mine of learning that is tapped through conversation.

## 4.
### CHECK OUT THE OTHER SIDE.

Take time to examine and understand another point of view, even if it radically contradicts yours. You may see things in a new light, or you may have your old convictions strengthened. Personal convictions that have never been tested remain flabby.

## 5.
### READ BROADLY.

Include a diversity of books, authors, and topics. Resist the temptation to read only those books that reinforce what you already believe.

## 6.
### KEEP A JOURNAL.

Recording what we learn captures our growth in wisdom.

## 7.
### EXPERIMENT.

Try new approaches and ideas. Age does not affect your ability to learn. An eighty-year-old can learn to surf the net like an eighteen-year-old.

## 8.
### APPLY WHAT YOU KNOW.

Our depth of understanding is often directly related to our ability to apply what we've learned. Application takes knowledge from the head to the heart.

BILL MOWRY
FROM "DISCIPLESHIP JOURNAL"

# YOUR FUTURE DEPENDS ON...

*Who you will be in the next five years*
*depends on three things:*

the books you read

the people you meet

the choices you make

*Choose today to live a transformed life!*

BOB AND EMILIE BARNES
FROM "THE 15-MINUTE MONEY MANAGER"

# WHAT IS SUCCESS?

*To laugh often and love much;*

*To win the respect of intelligent people and the affection of children;*

*To earn the approval of honest critics and
endure the betrayal of false friends;*

*To appreciate beauty;*

*To find the best in others;*

*To give of one's self;*

*To leave the world a bit better, whether by a healthy child,
a garden patch, or a redeemed social condition;*

*To have played and laughed with enthusiasm
and sung with exultation;*

*To know even one life has breathed easier because you have lived…*

*This is to have succeeded.*

RALPH WALDO EMERSON
POET, ESSAYIST, AND PHILOSOPHER

# FRIENDSHIP

*A heart for others*

2

# HINTS FOR A HAPPY FRIENDSHIP

### 1.
*Make friends even if you don't think you need them.*

### 2.
*Seek out quiet people. They have a lot to say, if you say something first.*

### 3.
*Don't establish a friendship based on mutual dislikes.*

### 4.
*Call if you're running late.*

### 5.
*Look people in the eye when you talk to them.*

### 6.
*Be one who says positive things about others.*

### 7.
*Learn to tell a good story.*

### 8.
*Ask other people about themselves.*

### 9.
*Be happy for others in their good fortune.*

### 10.
*Make sure your caring includes doing.*

### 11.
*Know when to say good-bye.*

BRUCE & CHERYL BICKEL AND STAN & KARIN JANTZ
FROM "LIFE'S LITTLE HANDBOOK OF WISDOM"

# HOW TO GET ALONG WITH PEOPLE

### 1.
LIKE. *If you genuinely like people, enjoy being with them, talking with them, and like being helpful to them, you will find that people generally will like you. And when mutual liking exists, people get along with one another.*

### 2.
INTEREST. *Become interested in the other person's ideas and activities. Direct conversation to the other individual's interests, rather than talking about yourself. As you become absorbed in his interests, he will become attentive to yours, and you will have a pleasant time together.*

### 3.
LIKABLE. *To be liked and to get along with people, it is necessary to be a likable person. Practice the old saying: "To have friends, be friendly."*

### 4.
NAMES. *Practice the art of remembering names. Focus on the other person, so that the name will register. Remember that a person's name is important to him. Knowing it will help you get along with him.*

### 5.
EASY. *Be easy to get along with. Be a comfortable sort of person, so that there is no strain in being with you. Be an "old shoe" kind of individual. Be homey, down to earth.*

### 6.
STIMULATING. *Cultivate the quality of being stimulating. If being with you makes people feel better and more alive, you will be sought after; people will want to be with you; your personal relations will be excellent.*

### 7.

SCRATCHY. *Personal relations deteriorate when a person has scratchy elements in his personality. That is to say, do not rub people the wrong way. Be untense and affable.*

### 8.

SENSITIVE. *Avoid being on edge and sensitive, so that you are easily hurt; for people instinctively shy off from the super-sensitive, fearing to arouse an unpleasant reaction. Avoid the temptation to react with hurt feelings, and you will get along with people.*

### 9.

HEAL. *Sincerely attempt to heal on an honest basis every misunderstanding that you may have with other individuals. Mentally and spiritually drain off your grievances, and maintain an attitude of goodwill with every human being.*

### 10.

DO. *Love people and do things for them. Perform unselfish and outgoing acts of friendship. Such sincere self-giving inevitably leads to pleasant personal relations. It is all summed up in a familiar Scripture admonition:* "Do for others what you want them to do for you." *(See Matthew 7:12; Luke 6:31.)*

NORMAN VINCENT PEALE
FROM "HELP YOURSELF WITH GOD'S HELP"

# CELEBRATE YOUR DIFFERENCES

## 10 AREAS IN WHICH PEOPLE ARE DIFFERENT

### 1.

*Extrovert or Introvert:* Extroverts love crowds while introverts would rather spend time in solitude or with a close friend. Extroverts are energized by people and introverts are worn out by people.

### 2.

*Leaper or Looker:* Leapers take risks; when they see an opportunity they want to jump on it before it's too late. Lookers are more cautious. They like to carefully check everything out before making a decision.

### 3.

*Outliner or Detailer:* Outliners have a general focus and look at the big picture. They think in terms of direction and getting things done. Detailers look at the nuts and bolts. Their concern is *how* to get things done.

### 4.

*Spender or Saver:* If spenders have extra money, they want to spend—on themselves, on others, on worthy causes, on anything. If savers have extra money, they want to put it away for a rainy day. They do not like to spend unless it's very important.

### 5.

*Planner or Flexer:* Planners love structure with everything organized and neatly packaged. They like schedules and deadlines. Flexers bend with the flow of life and take things as they come. They tend to be spontaneous and laid back. Loose ends don't bother them because they believe everything will work out.

### 6.

*Scurrier or Ambler:* Scurriers are always busy. Speed and efficiency are their watchwords—accomplish as much as you can as fast as you can. Amblers take their time and set their own pace. They might not do as much, but they enjoy what they do.

## 7.

*Thinker or Feeler:* Thinkers focus on facts and principles. They base decisions on objective data and tend to be task oriented. Feelers focus on people and emotions. They base decisions on subjective data and tend to be relationship oriented.

## 8.

*Dreamer or Worker:* Dreamers are creative people who love to come up with ideas. They are optimistic and oriented toward the future. Workers are practical. They like to take other people's ideas and make them happen. They tend to be realistic and focus on the present.

## 9.

*Collector or Tosser:* Collectors gather things. They hate to throw anything away because they know they just might need it sometime. Tossers get rid of things. They hate clutter and they insist that if you haven't used something recently, you probably never will.

## 10.

*Juggler or Holder:* Jugglers are multichanneled and can deal with many things simultaneously. Holders are singlechanneled and can only deal with one, maybe two, things at a time. If they try to do more, they become stressed and overwhelmed.

*We are all different and unique.*
*That creates balance, variety, and challenges in relationships.*
*Celebrate your differences; talk about them too.*

DR. STEVE STEPHENS
FROM "MARRIAGE: EXPERIENCE THE BEST"

# RATING YOURSELF AS A FRIEND

### 1.
*Do you reach out to others rather than always expect
that they will call or come to see you?
Do you reciprocate?*

### 2.
*When you meet others, are you open to the possibility that they may
become future allies, confidantes, best friends?*

### 3.
*Do you approach others with an attitude of acceptance and interest?*

### 4.
*Are you a good listener,
or do you claim more than your share of the airtime?*

### 5.
*Do you refuse to become the only nurturer in the relationship?*

### 6.
*Are you loyal, and do you guard your friends' secrets?*

### 7.
*Do you practice unsolicited acts of kindness?*

8.

*Do you live an authentic life based on your values and beliefs?*

9.

*Can you ask for and grant forgiveness?*

10.

*Can you listen when a friend tells you that you've hurt her,
or do you withdraw or get defensive?*

11.

*Do you encourage other people to develop their strengths
and graciously help them overcome weaknesses?*

12.

*Can you enjoy a friend's good fortune—whether in marriage,
motherhood, or career—even if you aren't on a parallel track?*

BRENDA HUNTER AND HOLLY LARSON
FROM "IN THE COMPANY OF FRIENDS"

# TO BE A GOOD FRIEND

### 1.
*Smile often; laugh aloud now and then; giggle, even.*

### 2.
*Become aware of several things that you especially enjoy.*
*Watch for others who enjoy those same things.*

### 3.
*Identify an acquaintance who has a need you can supply.*
*Offer yourself.*
*(Hint: Start with the obvious—your sister, spouse, neighbor...)*

### 4.
*Learn to enjoy being alone with yourself.*
*Identify what elements of living enrich your life.*
*Incorporate them in your daily routines. If you are happy being*
*with you, it's likely others will enjoy your company too!*

### 5.
*Forget what you give, and remember what you receive.*

### 6.
*Be the one who is there doing when others are saying,*
*"Is there anything I can do?"*

### 7.
*Listen—even in the silence.*

GLORIA GAITHER, SUE BUCHANAN, PEGGY BENSON, AND JOY MACKENZIE
FROM "FRIENDS THROUGH THICK AND THIN"

# WATCH WHAT YOU SAY

---

1.

*Never tell jokes that slander.*


2.

*Never criticize in public unless you:*
*have already expressed your disappointment with*
*the other person in private, have already taken*
*someone with you to discuss the grievance*
*with the person, and are absolutely convinced*
*that public reprimand is necessary and will be helpful.*


3.

*Never say anything about anyone in their absence*
*that you wouldn't say in their presence.*

MAX LUCADO
FROM "GOD CAME NEAR"

---

# HOW TO FORGIVE AND FORGET

TO FORGIVE ANOTHER IS THE GREATEST FAVOR
YOU CAN DO—FOR YOURSELF.

### 1.

*Take the initiative.* Don't wait for the other person to apologize.

### 2.

*If the forgiven person wants to reenter your life, it is fair to demand truthfulness.* He or she should be made to understand, to feel the hurt you've felt. Then you should expect a sincere promise that you won't be hurt that way again.

### 3.

*Be patient.* If the hurt is deep, you can't forgive in a single instant.

### 4.

*Forgive "retail," not "wholesale."* It is almost impossible to forgive someone for being a bad person. Instead, focus on the particular act that hurt you. (It might help to write it down.)

### 5.

*Don't expect too much.* To forgive doesn't mean you must renew a once-close relationship.

### 6.

*Discard your self-righteousness.* A victim is not a saint. You, too, will need forgiveness some day.

### 7.

*Separate anger from hate.* To dissolve your hate: Face your emotion and accept it as natural. Then discuss it, either with the object of your hatred (if you can do so without escalating the hatred) or with a trusted third party.

### 8.

*Forgive yourself.* This may be the hardest act of all. Candor is critical. Admit your fault. Relax your struggle to be perfect. Then be concrete and specific about what is bothering you. Your deed was evil. You are not.

LEWIS B. SMEDES
CONDENSED FROM "FORGIVE AND FORGET"

FRIENDSHIP

# 12 TIMES TO SAY "I'M SORRY"

When you…

1.

*Are wrong*

2.

*Are rude*

3.

*Are defensive*

4.

*Are impatient*

5.

*Are negative*

6.

*Are hurtful*

### 7.
*Are insensitive*

### 8.
*Are forgetful*

### 9.
*Are confused or confusing*

### 10.
*Have neglected, ignored, or overlooked
something important to one you love*

### 11.
*Have damaged or misused something that
is not yours (even if it was an accident)*

### 12.
*Have not said "I'm sorry" as sincerely
and quickly as the situation needed*

DR. STEVE STEPHENS
PSYCHOLOGIST AND SEMINAR SPEAKER

# MENDING A FRIENDSHIP

## 1
### LOCATE THE TROUBLE SPOT.

This is the diagnosis step. Look back and try to assess what has gone wrong. Where did the misunderstanding begin? How did we get into this vicious circle of put-downs?

## 2.
### APOLOGIZE WHEN YOU'RE WRONG.

All of us are wrong—plenty of times. It is foolish to let pride and insecurity keep us from saying so and patching up the friendship. Norman Vincent Peale writes, "A true apology is more than just acknowledgment of a mistake. It is recognition that something you have said or done has damaged a relationship—and that you *care* enough about the relationship to want it repaired and restored."

## 3.
### CHECK TO SEE IF YOUR NEUROSES ARE SPOILING YOUR FRIENDSHIPS.

If a large number of your close friendships go sour, you might do well to ask if your neurotic patterns of relating are causing the problem.

## 4.
### CHECK TO SEE IF YOU EMPLOY OLD METHODS
### OF RELATING THAT NO LONGER WORK.

Each of us has emotional needs, and along the way each of us has acquired a bagful of tricks for getting those needs met. Unfortunately, we can learn some very neurotic ways of meeting those needs, and those neurotic patterns can get us into trouble again and again.

## 5.
### CHECK TO SEE IF YOU HAVE EXCESSIVE NEED FOR APPROVAL.

The better a man's self-image, the better friends he is likely to choose, hence the better the relationship, and hence his self-esteem is enhanced. The worse a man's self-image, the more likely he is to choose jerks for friends, hence the relationship is likely to go bad, and his self-image is further lowered because of this failure. So the lesson is obvious: You cannot depend on others for your sense of self-worth. It must come from within you.

ALAN LOY MCGINNIS
CONDENSED FROM "THE FRIENDSHIP FACTOR"

# IF YOU'RE GOING TO FIGHT...

*Fight for the relationship—not against it!*

*Fight for reconciliation—not for alienation.*

*Fight to preserve the friendship—not to destroy it.*

*Fight to win your spouse—not to lose him/her.*

*Fight to save your marriage—not to cash it in.*

*Fight to solve the problem—not to salve your ego.*

*If you're going to fight, fight to win…not to lose!*

DR. RICHARD C. HALVERSON, FORMER CHAPLAIN TO THE UNITED STATES SENATE
FROM "SOMEHOW INSIDE ETERNITY"

# HOW TO BUILD A FRIENDSHIP WITH SOMEONE YOU'RE DATING

**1.**
*Keep physical contact to a minimum.*

**2.**
*Explore new interests and hobbies.*

**3.**
*Do activities that are fun.*

**4.**
*Be yourself—don't put on an act just to get the person to like you.*

**5.**
*Ask open-ended questions.*

**6.**
*Listen to the other person's heart, not just to the words.*

**7.**
*Talk with a godly older couple and discover
how they built their friendship.*

**8.**
*Read a good book together, and discuss how its content
can help you foster your relationship.*

**9.**
*Seek to understand the other person's viewpoint.*

REMEMBER THAT THE MORE YOU KNOW ABOUT EACH OTHER BEFORE
MARRIAGE, THE FEWER NEGATIVE SURPRISES THERE WILL BE AFTER THE WEDDING

DICK PURNELL
FROM "DECISION" MAGAZINE

# FINDING A LISTENING EAR

IN CHOOSING A CONFIDANT, YOU SHOULD LOOK FOR:

*someone you trust*

*someone who can keep a confidence*

*someone who will respect your boundaries*

*someone who will give you perspective*

*someone who will pray for you*

*someone who is wise and has more experience than you*

*someone who values commitment in marriage*

*someone who will keep you accountable
without unjustly condemning you*

*someone of the same sex, or a married couple*

*someone who will not be negatively affected by your confidences.*

JANIS LONG HARRIS
FROM "MARRIAGE PARTNERSHIP" MAGAZINE

# KEEPING A CONFIDENCE

When you're making progress toward developing an intimate friendship, it's crucial that you keep a confidence. Nothing will ruin a potential relationship quicker than a loose tongue. The only information you should be revealing to a third party is the type that passes the following criteria:

### 1.
*Is it true?*

### 2.
*Is it kind?*

### 3.
*Is it necessary to tell?*

### 4.
*Is it beneficial to all concerned?*

### 5.
*Do you have the other person's permission to share the story?*

Use these five questions as your rule of thumb when you're tempted to divulge someone else's business. If the answer to any or all of these five questions is no, you're just asking for trouble if you pass it along.

JOANNA WALLACE AND DEANNA WALLACE
FROM "ESPECIALLY FOR A WOMAN"

# 10 WAYS TO WELCOME
# A NEW NEIGHBOR

### 1.

*Acknowledge that you see them moving in,* whether it is a wave of your hand from your yard or a quick "Welcome to the neighborhood. I'm looking forward to getting to know you."

### 2.

*Resist the urge to stand at your window* while they unload.

### 3.

*A plate of cookies or a pot of stew* can be most appreciated at their front door but don't go in unless invited. Then stay only a few minutes unless your help is welcome.

### 4.

*When you finish with it, leave your copy of the newspaper* in their box or on their porch for the first week.

### 5.

*If the new neighbors are from out of town, a packet made up of a city map, a list of local events, museums, concerts, etc., might be really welcome.* Or, with their permission, give their name and address to a local welcoming service.

### 6.

*Blending kindness with firmness, make your boundaries known* if the new neighbor's children or pets begin to violate your space. If you don't complain about their dog pottying in your yard when it first begins, the habit will become difficult to break.

### 7.

*Tell neighbors to let you know if they need recommendations* for shopping, a dentist, dry cleaners, etc., rather than just volunteering them.

### 8.

*Never be critical* of the people who used to live there.

### 9.

*After two weeks, a neighborhood dessert or potluck dinner* can introduce newcomers to other people who live nearby.

### 10.

*If your offer of help or friendship is refused, don't push.* Wait until your neighbors have time to get settled and look *you* over. In the meantime, smile.

BARBARA BAUMGARDNER
AUTHOR AND SPEAKER

# NURTURING LONG-DISTANCE FRIENDSHIPS

*Choose a specific time of day when you can commit to
praying for each other.*

*Send photos! Not just the kids' school pictures, but
photos of anything important in your life—
a new hairstyle, your latest gardening or remodeling project,
your children's everyday antics, new friends.*

*Create a code between the two of you that says,
"I'm thinking of you—you're special."
Maybe it's a particular greeting or closing to your letters.*

*Always send a birthday card—unless
you've agreed ahead of time not to do cards.*

*Make it a habit to hit that reply button on the e-mail,
even if it's just a short note.
Don't wait so long between letters
that it takes a novel to catch up on your life.*

*Never underestimate the effectiveness of the oft-maligned
Christmas newsletter to keep friends up-to-date.
Just don't send the newsletter to everyone.*

*Talk about your friend to others.
Saying her name out loud and "introducing" her to
others keeps your friendship alive.*

*If you're on e-mail, send a "real letter" every once in a while—
something pretty or a funny card or even a comic from
the newspaper that made you laugh.*

*Create your own traditions.
My mom and her best friend sent each other the same birthday card
for years. They added a personal letter each birthday and
kept that special card in a safe place the rest of the year.*

*Embrace when you finally see each other again!*

RENÉE S. SANFORD
RENÉE LIVES IN THE UNITED STATES—HER BEST FRIEND LIVES IN EUROPE

# WHAT IS LOVE?

### 1.

*Love delights in giving attention rather than attracting it.*

### 2.

*Love finds the element of good and builds on it.*

### 3.

*Love does not magnify defects.*

### 4.

*Love is a flame that warms but never burns.*

### 5.

*Love knows how to disagree without becoming disagreeable.*

### 6.

*Love rejoices at the success of others instead of being envious.*

FATHER JAMES KELLER, FOUNDER, THE CHRISTOPHERS
AS CITED IN "MORE OF...THE BEST OF BITS & PIECES," ROB GILBERT, PH.D., ED.

# VIRTUE
## *Marks of character*

3

# DESTINY

Watch your thoughts; they become words.

Watch your words; they become actions.

Watch your actions; they become habits.

Watch your habits; they become character.

Watch your character; it becomes your destiny.

FRANK OUTLAW
AS CITED IN "MORE OF...THE BEST OF BITS & PIECES," ROB GILBERT, PH.D., ED.

VIRTUE

# 20 GIFTS TO GIVE

1.
*Mend a quarrel.*

2.
*Seek out a forgotten friend.*

3.
*Hug someone tightly and whisper, "I love you so."*

4.
*Forgive an enemy.*

5.
*Be gentle and patient with an angry person.*

6.
*Express appreciation.*

7.
*Gladden the heart of a child.*

8.
*Find the time to keep a promise.*

9.
*Make or bake something for someone else. Anonymously.*

10.
*Speak kindly to a stranger.*

11.
*Enter into another's sorrow.*

### 12.
*Smile. Laugh a little. Laugh a little more.*

### 13.
*Take a walk with a friend.*

### 14.
*Kneel down and pat a dog.*

### 15.
*Lessen your demands on others.*

### 16.
*Apologize if you were wrong.*

### 17.
*Turn off the television and talk.*

### 18.
*Pray for someone who helped you when you hurt.*

### 19.
*Give a soft answer even though you feel strongly.*

### 20.
*Encourage an older person.*

CHARLES R. SWINDOLL
CONDENSED FROM "THE FINISHING TOUCH"

# ACTIONS THAT TAKE COURAGE

*Admitting you are wrong.*

*Doing what is right when everyone else isn't.*

*Speaking to someone you don't know.*

*Saying "no" when people are trying to get you to do
something you know you shouldn't.*

*Telling the truth and accepting the consequences.*

*Standing up for something you believe in even though
it might mean rejection or ridicule or even physical harm.*

*Defending someone who is considered unpopular or unacceptable.*

*Facing a limitation and giving it your very best
regardless of pain or discomforts.*

Confronting a fear without running away.

Giving sacrificially to protect or promote either
someone you love, someone who has been wronged,
or someone who is in need.

Being the only one.

Taking a risk.

Sharing your heart honestly
(including your feelings and fears and failures).

Living your faith with all your heart, mind, soul, and
strength regardless of the cost.

DR. STEVE STEPHENS
PSYCHOLOGIST AND SEMINAR SPEAKER

VIRTUE

# BENJAMIN FRANKLIN'S 13 VIRTUES

## 1.
### TEMPERANCE

*Eat not to dullness; drink not to elevation.*

## 2.
### SILENCE

*Speak not but what may benefit others or yourself;avoid trifling conversation.*

## 3.
### ORDER

*Let all your things have their places; let each part of your business have its time.*

## 4.
### RESOLUTION

*Resolve to perform what you ought; perform without fail what you resolve.*

## 5.
### FRUGALITY

*Make no expense but to do good to others or yourself; i.e., waste nothing.*

## 6.
### INDUSTRY

*Lose no time; be always employed in something useful; cut off all unnecessary actions.*

## 7.
### SINCERITY

*Use no hurtful deceit; think innocently and justly; and, if you speak, speak accordingly.*

## 8.
### JUSTICE

*Wrong none by doing injuries, or omitting the benefits that are your duty.*

## 9.
### MODERATION

*Avoid extremes; forbear resenting injuries so much as you think they deserve.*

## 10.
### CLEANLINESS

*Tolerate no uncleanliness in body, clothes, or habitation.*

## 11.
### TRANQUILLITY

*Be not disturbed by trifles or at accidents common or unavoidable.*

## 12.
### CHASTITY

*Rarely use venery but for health or offspring, never to dullness, weakness, or the injury of your own or another's peace or reputation.*

## 13.
### HUMILITY

*Imitate Jesus and Socrates.*

PETER SHAW, ED.
FROM "THE AUTOBIOGRAPHY AND OTHER WRITINGS BY BENJAMIN FRANKLIN"

VIRTUE

# WHAT I BELIEVE IN AND VALUE

### GRACE
*Treasure life as a gift from God.*

### STRENGTH/FORTITUDE
*Fight the good fight, hard.*

### LOVE
*Embrace people with openness and acceptance.*

### HOPE
*Facilitate the growth and success of others.*

### HUMAN DIGNITY
*Seek first to understand before passing judgment.*

### BEING REAL (INTEGRITY)
*Acquire enough wisdom to be humble.*

### FUN
*Have at least one hearty laugh each day.*

### IMPACT
*Practice the courage to take risks.*

CHARLIE HEDGES
CONDENSED FROM "GETTING THE RIGHT THINGS RIGHT"

# PEOPLE WITH CHARACTER

*They walk with integrity.*

*They do what is right.*

*They tell the truth.*

*They don't gossip.*

*They don't mistreat people.*

*They side with those who are right.*

*They keep their word.*

*They lend money to those in need without interest.*

*They don't take advantage of people for financial gain.*

ADAPTED FROM THE PSALMS
COMPILED BY ANDREW STANLEY FROM "A DIAMOND IN THE ROUGH"

VIRTUE

# 10 REASONS FOR GOING TO CHURCH

*Teddy Roosevelt offered his reasons for going to church in*
Ladies' Home Journal *in 1917:*

## 1.

In this actual world a churchless community, a community where men have abandoned and scoffed at or ignored their religious needs, is a community on the rapid downgrade.

## 2.

Church work and church attendance mean the cultivation of the habit of feeling some responsibility for others and the sense of braced moral strength which prevents a relaxation of one's own moral fiber.

## 3.

There are enough holidays for most of us which can quite properly be devoted to pure holiday making... Sundays differ from other holidays—among other ways—in the fact that there are fifty-two of them every year.... On Sunday, go to church.

## 4.

Yes, I know all the excuses. I know that one can worship the Creator and dedicate oneself to good living in a grove of trees, or by a running brook, or in one's own house, just as well as in church. But I also know as a matter of cold fact the average man does not thus worship or thus dedicate himself. If he stays away from church he does not spend his time in good works or in lofty meditation. He looks over the colored supplement of the newspaper.

### 5.

He may not hear a good sermon at church. But unless he is very unfortunate he will hear a sermon by a good man who, with his good wife, is engaged all the week long in a series of wearing and humdrum and important tasks for making hard lives a little easier.

### 6.

He will listen to and take part in reading some beautiful passages from the Bible. And if he is not familiar with the Bible, he has suffered a loss....

### 7.

He will probably take part in singing some good hymns.

### 8.

He will meet and nod to, or speak to, good, quiet neighbors.... He will come away feeling a little more charitably toward all the world, even toward those excessively foolish young men who regard church-going as rather a soft performance.

### 9.

I advocate a man's joining in church works for the sake of showing his faith by his works.

### 10.

The man who does not in some way, active or not, connect himself with some active, working church misses many opportunities for helping his neighbors, and therefore, incidentally, for helping himself.

THEODORE ROOSEVELT
TWENTY-SIXTH PRESIDENT OF THE UNITED STATES

# A PRAYER FOR EVERYONE

---

*From the cowardice that shrinks from new truth,*

*From the laziness that's content with half-truth,*

*From the arrogance from the one who thinks he knows all truth,*

*Oh God of truth,*

*Deliver me!*

AN ANCIENT PRAYER

---

# EXTREME VIRTUES

Truth, if it becomes a weapon against persons.

Beauty, if it becomes a vanity.

Love, if it becomes possessive.

Loyalty, if it becomes blind, careless trust.

Tolerance, if it becomes indifference.

Self-confidence, if it becomes arrogance.

Faith, if it becomes self-righteousness.

ASHLEY COOPER, COLUMNIST
AS CITED IN "MORE OF...THE BEST OF BITS & PIECES," ROB GILBERT, PH.D., ED.

# THE ADVENTURE OF GIVING

### ANONYMOUS GIVING

*Listen for specific needs people have and then
figure out a way to meet them undetected.*

### PLANNING FOR ANNUAL GIFTS

*Every spring I anticipate several one-time gift appeals
for summer missions opportunities.
I set aside money so that I can respond to as many as possible.*

### TAKING SOMEONE SHOPPING

*Rather than just handing someone money, take them shopping.*

### HIRING FOR SERVICES

*I know a talented single mom on a meager income.
I "commission" her to make floral arrangements for me.
She earns extra money with dignity, and I get hand-crafted decorations.*

### FOOTING THE BILL

*Pay some of the tuition, or cover for the textbooks, or supply
the paper and pens, for someone going back to school.*

### RECYCLING THINGS YOU DON'T NEED

*A friend of mine recently upgraded to a new computer system.
Rather than selling her old system, she gave it to a high school student
with the promise of tutoring her in word processing skills.*

### GIVING AS A FAMILY

*Many families have rediscovered the joy of the holidays by
pooling the money they'd normally spend on each other
and getting gifts for people less fortunate.*

### JUST 'CUZ GIFTS

*Giving gifts for no apparent reason is a creative way to express
care and love, especially when you give them in unusual ways.*

BECKY BRODIN
FROM "DISCIPLESHIP JOURNAL"

# KINDNESS

Be kind and merciful.

Let no one ever come to you

without leaving better and happier.

Be a living expression of God's kindness.

Kindness in your face,

Kindness in your eyes,

Kindness in your smile,

Kindness in your warm greeting.

MOTHER TERESA
FOUNDER OF MISSIONARIES OF CHARITY

# RULES FOR CHRISTIAN LIVING

*Do all the good you can,*

*By all the means you can,*

*In all the ways you can,*

*In all the places you can,*

*At all the times you can,*

*To all the people you can,*

*As long as ever...*

*...you can!*

JOHN WESLEY
EVANGELIST AND THEOLOGIAN

# MORAL GUIDANCE
# FOR YOUR FAMILY

## YOU CAN MAKE A DIFFERENCE!

### 1.
*Do what is morally right.*
Be a role model, and act with authority.

### 2.
*Choose good, and reject the mediocre and evil.*
Now is the time to rid your household of any reading or viewing
material you know to be vulgar, offensive, or morally confusing.

### 3.
*Bring into your home only things you know to be interesting, educational,*
*entertaining, AND edifying.* Leave magazines and books around
where your child will be enticed to pick them up and browse.

### 4.
*The TV and remote belong to you.*
You hold the power! Get your children accustomed to
asking permission before watching TV or selected videos.

### 5.
*Your home is your castle.*
What you have on display or allow to be viewed
represents *you.* "Would God be pleased?" is a good
guide in judging material allowed in the home.

### 6.
*Don't let teens or young adults bully you.*
Gently but firmly remind them that until they are in their own home,
they have no right to air a program you consider objectionable.

### 7.
*Don't allow TV sets in children's bedrooms.*
They cause isolation and can promote unlimited
or unhealthy viewing habits.

### 8.
*Be consistent.*
Don't confuse a child with changed minds or plea bargaining
in the area of material you know to be vulgar or immoral.

### 9.
*Set the tone.*
Viewing graphically violent or sexually explicit material invades
a youngster's imagination and may confuse his or her thinking.

### 10.
*Be fair.*
Tell your youngster beforehand, then stick to your rules.

### 11.
*Don't give in or give up.*
If setting media standards is new at your house, be patient, yet firm.

MARY ANN KUHARSKI, FREELANCE WRITER, HOMEMAKER, AND MOTHER OF 13
CONDENSED FROM "HOMELIFE" MAGAZINE

# THE 10 COMMANDMENTS

### 1.
*Do not worship any other gods besides me.*

### 2.
*Do not make idols of any kind.*

### 3.
*Do not misuse the name of the Lord your God.*

### 4.
*Remember to observe the Sabbath day by keeping it holy.*

### 5.
*Honor your father and mother.*

### 6.
*Do not murder.*

### 7.
*Do not commit adultery.*

### 8.
*Do not steal.*

### 9.
*Do not testify falsely against your neighbor.*

### 10.
*Do not covet your neighbor's house or anything else your neighbor owns.*

FROM "THE HOLY BIBLE"
NEW LIVING TRANSLATION

# SEVEN DEADLY WRONGS

1.

*Wealth without work*

2.

*Pleasure without conscience*

3.

*Knowledge without character*

4.

*Science without humanity*

5.

*Commerce without morality*

6.

*Worship without sacrifice*

7.

*Politics without principle*

AUTHOR UNKNOWN

# FAITH

I believe in the sun, even though it doesn't shine,

I believe in love, even when it isn't shown,

I believe in God, even when he doesn't speak.

FOUND ON THE WALL OF A CONCENTRATION CAMP

# LIFE'S TRANSITIONS

*Passages through the years*

4

# THINGS TO FEEL NOSTALGIC ABOUT

*A barefoot walk along a sandy beach.*

*A quiet visit to the place you were raised.*

*Listening to a rippling brook running over the rocks*

*through a forest of autumn leaves.*

*Singing the song of your alma mater.*

*Looking over childhood photos in the family album.*

*Watching your now-grown "child" leave home.*

*Standing silently beside the grave of a close,*

*personal friend or relative.*

*The smell and sounds of a warm fireplace.*

*An old letter, bruised with age, signed by one who loved you.*

*Climbing to the top of a wind-swept hill.*

*Getting alone—all alone—and reading aloud.*

*Christmas Eve, late at night.*

*Certain poems…certain melodies.*

*Weddings…graduations…diplomas.*

*Snow…sleds…toboggans.*

*Saying good-bye.*

CHARLES R. SWINDOLL
FROM "GROWING STRONG IN THE SEASONS OF LIFE"

# LIFE'S LESSONS

## WISDOM THROUGH THE AGES

I've learned that I like my teacher because she cries when we sing "Silent Night." (Age 6)

I've learned that you can't hide a piece of broccoli in a glass of milk. (Age 7)

I've learned that when I wave to people in the country, they stop what they are doing and wave back. (Age 9)

I've learned that if you want to cheer yourself up, you should try cheering someone else up. (Age 14)

I've learned that although it's hard to admit it, I'm secretly glad my parents are strict with me. (Age 15)

I've learned that silent company is often more healing than words of advice. (Age 24)

I've learned that if someone says something unkind about me, I must live so that no one will believe it. (Age 39)

I've learned that the greater a person's sense of guilt, the greater his need to cast blame on others. (Age 46)

I've learned that singing "Amazing Grace" can lift my spirits for hours. (Age 49)

I've learned that you can tell a lot about a man by the way he handles these three things: a rainy day, lost luggage, and tangled Christmas tree lights. (Age 52)

I've learned that regardless of your relationship with your parents, you miss them terribly after they die. (Age 53)

I've learned that if you want to do something positive for your children, try to improve your marriage. (Age 61)

I've learned that life sometimes gives you a second chance. (Age 62)

I've learned that if you pursue happiness, it will elude you. But if you focus on your family, the needs of others, your work, meeting new people, and doing the very best you can, happiness will find you. (Age 65)

I've learned that whenever I decide something with kindness, I usually make the right decision. (Age 66)

I've learned that everyone can use a prayer. (Age 72)

I've learned that even when I have pains, I don't have to be one. (Age 82)

I've learned that every day you should reach out and touch someone. People love human touch—holding hands, a warm hug, or just a friendly pat on the back. (Age 85)

I've learned that I still have a lot to learn. (Age 92)

SELECTED

# DON'T LET YOUR NEW BABY DRIVE YOU APART

### 1.

"The greatest thing parents can do for their children is to love each other," advises Dr. Benjamin Salk, family psychologist.

### 2.

While giving your baby as much love as you can, be careful about protecting your own privacy. At times you'll want to let your baby share your bed, but be cautious as to how often. If space allows, let the baby sleep in a separate room as soon as possible.

### 3.

Have conversations that are not dominated by the latest in baby foods and teething rings.

### 4.

Realize how easy it is for the father to feel both unneeded and excluded.

### 5.

Share as many tasks as possible, even if this means they are not done to perfection. The baby will survive with a crooked diaper.

## 6.

Recognize how physically shattered many women become with the sheer effort of looking after a small baby.

## 7.

If sex is not at the top of the agenda for a while, make sure this is not confused with rejection, and try to show intimacy in other ways.

## 8.

Don't lose touch with your friends.

## 9.

Don't refuse to let trusted friends look after your child for a few hours.

## 10.

As the child grows, keep a sense of moderation in terms of his involvement in extra activities. You can exhaust yourselves and your child quite easily.

ROB PARSONS
CONDENSED FROM "THE 60-MINUTE MARRIAGE BUILDER"

# COUNTDOWN TO COLLEGE

### DEFINE EXPECTATIONS

• Talk honestly about the temptation of putting new interests and friends ahead of studies. Be encouraging but firm about the importance of time management.

• Holidays and vacation times in the year ahead will no doubt offer opportunities for new cultural experiences. Discuss which holidays you expect your child to spend at home. Don't forget to talk about opportunities for your child to bring friends home to visit.

### DETERMINE A BUDGET

• Whether your freshman will be working or receiving a monthly allowance, sit down together and determine a livable budget. As you're crunching numbers, don't forget to include the phone bill, clothing and personal items, as well as gas and maintenance for a vehicle (if applicable).

• Open a checking account early in the summer to foster familiarity with banking processes. Make sure your child understands how to balance a checkbook.

## KEEP THE LINES OF COMMUNICATION OPEN

• A college post-office box can be the loneliest spot on campus. Try to keep your freshman's box filled by sending cards and letters as often as possible. Why not surprise him or her with a favorite magazine subscription?

• Decide how often you will communicate by telephone. Once your freshman is settled on campus, let him or her set a regular time for calling home—and then make sure you're 100 percent available when he or she calls.

KATHY CHAPMAN SHARP AND REBEKAH D. SHARP
FROM "HOMELIFE" MAGAZINE

# WHEN YOUR ADULT CHILDREN WANT TO MOVE BACK HOME

## 1.
### BE IN AGREEMENT.

Before you take anyone into your home, agree with your mate to stand together on decisions. If one partner is strongly opposed to the return of the adult child (with or without a family), the situation will never work.

## 2.
### ESTABLISH CONTROL.

If your children come back home, clearly spell out whose home it is. When your kids show the first sign of bucking for control, both parents must take quick action.

## 3.
### SET A TIME LIMIT RIGHT FROM THE START.

Don't let anyone move in for an indefinite time.

## 4.
### ASSIGN JOBS.

Don't start doing their laundry and making their beds. You already raised your family once; you don't need to do it a second time.

## 5.
### KEEP YOUR REGULAR MEALTIMES.

If your guests want to eat at separate times or don't like what you cook, make it clear they can buy their own food, cook it, and clean up afterwards.

## 6.
### LET THEM KNOW THIS ISN'T A HOTEL.

Not only should mealtimes be established and cleanup assigned, but guests must not expect hotel services. You should not be in charge of their business calls, their dry cleaning, or their change of linens.

## 7.
### MAKE THEM CONTRIBUTE FINANCIALLY.

Granting family members a week or two of hospitality can be considered a kind gift, but if signs reveal this visit will be longer, establish a time frame and ask them to share the expenses.

## 8.
### DON'T LET THEM CRITICIZE.

Right from the start, let them know that if they don't like your home, your lifestyle, or your friends, they can leave.

## 9.
### DON'T USE THE CHILDREN AS A DUMPING GROUND.

Often when grandchildren move in, Grandma and Grandpa use them to express the feelings they don't dare say to the parents.

## 10.
### DON'T ASSUME GUILT.

One young couple complained when their parents didn't always want to babysit so they could go out more. The parents stated calmly but clearly, "We did not have these babies; you did. We love them, but we are not responsible for their care. When we babysit, it is a gift of love."

FLORENCE LITTAUER
ADAPTED FROM "WAKE UP, WOMEN!"

# PREPARING FOR RETIREMENT

### 1.
*Speak to people who are already retired.*

### 2.
*Reevaluate priorities.*

### 3.
*Determine what legacy you wish to leave.*

### 4.
*Reassess finances and plan your future.*

### 5.
*Begin downsizing if necessary.*

### 6.
*Develop new hobbies.*

### 7.
*Do more things with your spouse.*

### 8.
*Look for volunteer activities.*

### 9.
*Plan future vacations.*

### 10.
*Think of classes you might want to take.*

### 11.
*Set up an exercise program.*

### 12.
*Increase time with special friends and start
developing new friends with similar interests.*

ALICE GRAY, DR. STEVE STEPHENS, AND JOHN VAN DIEST

# FOUR WAYS TO GROW OLD GRACEFULLY

1.
*Fear less; hope more.*

2.
*Eat less; chew more.*

3.
*Talk less; say more.*

4.
*Hate less; love more.*

ABIGAIL VAN BUREN
FROM "THE OREGONIAN"

# STAY YOUNG WHILE GROWING OLD

**1.**

*Applaud others' successes.*

**2.**

*Exercise daily.*

**3.**

*Keep a positive attitude.*

**4.**

*Read widely and often.*

**5.**

*Play with children.*

**6.**

*Enjoy nature.*

**7.**

*Laugh heartily.*

**8.**

*Take a class.*

**9.**

*Plant a garden.*

## 10.

*Count your blessings.*

## 11.

*Take risks.*

## 12.

*Sing from your heart.*

## 13.

*Get a pet.*

## 14.

*Eat healthy.*

## 15.

*Give generously to others.*

TRESS VAN DIEST
89 YEARS YOUNG

# IF I HAD IT TO DO OVER AGAIN

*I would love my wife more in front of my children.*

*I would laugh with my children more—at our mistakes and our joys.*

*I would listen more—even to the youngest child.*

*I would be more honest about my own
weaknesses and stop pretending perfection.*

*I would pray differently for my family.*

*I would do more things with my children.*

*I would be more encouraging and bestow more praise.*

*I would pay more attention to little things,
deeds, and words of love and kindness.*

*Finally, if I had to do it all over again, I would share God
more intimately with my family. I would use ordinary
things that happened in every ordinary day to point them to God.*

AUTHOR UNKNOWN

# TOUGH QUESTIONS TO ASK ELDERLY PARENTS

### 1.

*Do you have up-to-date wills?*

### 2.

*Do you have hidden assets or liabilities?*

### 3.

*Where do you keep your important financial documents?*

### 4.

*Who will handle your affairs if you become incapacitated?*

### 5.

*Do you have a living will and a medical power of attorney?*

### 6.

*Do you have sufficient medical insurance?*

### 7.

*Do you have long-term care insurance?*

### 8.

*Have you made funeral plans?*

### 9.

*Will your estate owe taxes, and do you have money to pay them?*

FINANCIAL LITERACY CENTER
FROM "NEW MAN" MAGAZINE

# HOW ADULT CHILDREN
# CAN HELP THEIR PARENTS

### 1.
#### COMMUNICATE OFTEN.

*Keep in touch by telephone, visits, and letters.
Remember holidays, birthdays, and anniversaries.*

### 2.
#### RESPECT INDEPENDENCE.

*As long as possible, your parents need to make their
own decisions about where and how to live.*

### 3.
#### SUPPORT "LETTING GO."

*Help them find constructive ways to dispose of possessions by alerting
them to thrift stores or mission programs that can benefit from
their contributions. Listen to them and weep with them when they must
give up their homes, their driver's licenses, or their leadership positions.*

### 4.
#### EMPATHIZE WITH THEM.

*If you were in their place, how would you act and feel?*

### 5.
#### ENCOURAGE REMINISCING.

*Draw forth memories of the past and help them
fit together the pieces of their experiences.*

## 6.
### LISTEN TO THEM.

*Hear the accounts of their past disappointments, accomplishments, and satisfactions—even if told repeatedly—as well as the accounts of their current worries and fears, joys and hopes and delights.*

## 7.
### ENCOURAGE SPIRITUAL GROWTH.

*Help them find large-print Bibles, enriching TV and radio programs, and transportation to attend church. Encourage them to join a prayer chain or a service group.*

## 8.
### SUPPORT USEFULNESS.

*Seek their counsel, praise their hobbies, and encourage their giving service to others.*

## 9.
### STIMULATE THEIR SOCIAL LIFE.

*Encourage them to maintain old social relationships and to make new ones. "For none of us lives to himself alone and none of us dies to himself alone."*

## 10.
### PRAY FOR THEM AND WITH THEM.

*Their physical, mental, social, and material well-being is interconnected with their spiritual health.*

DAVID O. MOBERG
FROM "DECISION MAGAZINE"

# QUESTIONS PARENTS SHOULD ASK BEFORE MOVING IN WITH THEIR CHILDREN

### 1.

Do you really want to live with your son or daughter? Do they want you to live with them?

### 2.

Can your family afford to have you live with them? Can you help with household expenses?

### 3.

How easily can you adapt to your family's lifestyle and they to yours? Will you feel like a visitor in their home?

### 4.

What are the strengths and weaknesses of your relationship with your children (and their spouses)?

### 5.

Can you continue to pursue hobbies you enjoy? Can you keep in touch with your friends?

### 6.

How much time do you expect your family to spend with you? If you are home alone during the day, will you feel isolated or depressed?

## 7.

Will you have your own room? Can you bring along a favorite chair? Are there stairs to climb?

## 8.

Can you keep your car and driver's license? Are you willing and able to ride a bus or do you need to depend on your family for transportation?

## 9.

Can you help with the cooking and cleaning? Do you want to? Will your family let you?

## 10.

Will you need help with your personal care? If you will, can your family accommodate your needs?

## 11.

If you can't manage your own financial affairs, who will assume this responsibility?

# NURSING HOME CHECKLIST

1.
What are the facility's admission requirements?

2.
Are the staff kind and do they show respect to the residents?

3.
Are most residents dressed for the season and time of day?

4.
Do the staff know the residents by name?

5.
Do the staff respond quickly to resident calls for assistance?

6.
Are activities tailored to residents' individual needs and interests?

7.
Does the home use care in selecting roommates?

8.
Does the home have enough help on weekends and night shifts?

9.
Does the facility have contact with community groups,
such as churches, pet therapy programs, or Scouts?

10.
Does the resident or his or her family participate in
developing the resident's care plan?

11.
Does the home offer on-sight programs to restore lost physical functioning (for
example, physical therapy, occupational therapy, speech and language therapy)?

**12.**
Does the home have the special services that meet your needs? For example, special care units for residents with dementia or with respiratory problems?

**13.**
Is a registered nurse available for nursing staff and do they have an arrangement with a nearby hospital?

**14.**
Is the facility certified for government health insurance?

**15.**
Are there outdoor areas accessible for resident use?

**16.**
Is the inside of the nursing home clean and free from unpleasant odors?

**17.**
Are there private areas for residents to visit with family, visitors, or physicians?

**18.**
Does the nursing home have a good reputation in the community?

**19.**
Is the facility close for family or friends to visit?

**20.**
Does the home have a staff physician who systematically calls on the residents?

DAN GRADY, CHAPLAIN
NURSING HOME MINISTRIES

# A ROAD MAP THROUGH GRIEF

### 1.
*Pace yourself.*

### 2.
*Lean into the pain.*

### 3.
*Get ready for a second wave of grief.*

### 4.
*Trust the recovery process.*

### 5.
*Welcome help from those who love you.*

### 6.
*Protect your physical health.*

### 7.
*Refuse to live with regrets.*

### 8.
*Avoid major changes.*

### 9.
*Look beyond people's words.*

### 10.
*Let your grief benefit others.*

MARY A. WHITE
FROM "HARSH GRIEF, GENTLE HOPE"

# RECOVERY FROM GRIEF

YOU WILL KNOW YOU'RE BEGINNING TO RECOVER WHEN:

*Taking care of yourself is not only okay, but it feels good.*

*The future is not so frightening.*

*You can handle "special days" without falling apart.*

*You want to reach out to others in need or in pain.*

*Your emotional roller coaster is slowing down.*

*You skip or forget a ritual, such as visiting the cemetery, without grief.*

SISTER TERESA MCINTIER,, CSI, RNM, MB
FROM "YOU'LL KNOW YOU ARE RECOVERING WHEN..."

# HEAVEN IS A PLACE...

With no hunger.

With no thirst.

With no tears.

With no death.

With no sadness.

With no pain.

With no hard labor.

That is beautiful.

That is magnificent.

JAY CARTY
CONDENSED FROM "PLAYING THE ODDS"

# MARRIAGE

*Experiencing the best*

5

# 18 ATTRIBUTES TO LOOK FOR IN A MARRIAGE PARTNER

1. Positive attitude

2. Spiritual values

3. Sense of humor

4. Faithfulness

5. Honesty

6. Respect

7. Good communication skills

8. Hard working

9. Compassionate

10. Playful

11. Generous

12. Forgiving

13. Flexible

14. Confident

15. Sensitive

16. Understanding

17. Common sense

18. Money-wise

AL AND ALICE GRAY
MARRIED 32 YEARS AND MORE IN LOVE EVERY DAY

# WHAT KEEPS A MARRIAGE STRONG?

IN MY TWENTY YEARS OF FAMILY COUNSELING,
HERE ARE THE TOP REASONS COUPLES
HAVE GIVEN ME FOR STAYING TOGETHER:

*My spouse is my best friend.*

*We enjoy our time together.*

*I like my spouse as a person.*

*Marriage is a lifelong commitment.*

*My spouse is interested in me as a person.*

*Marriage is sacred.*

*We have common dreams and goals.*

*Children need a stable home.*

*My spouse is positive and builds me up.*

*I want the relationship to succeed.*

*We respect and appreciate each other.*

*My spouse encourages my personal growth.*

*We laugh together.*

*I trust my spouse.*

*We have a positive sexual life.*

*We have built a secure and comfortable life together.*

*My spouse accepts me for who I am.*

*We have similar beliefs and interests.*

*We communicate well.*

*I respect my spouse.*

DR. STEVE STEPHENS
PSYCHOLOGIST AND SEMINAR SPEAKER

# HIS NEEDS, HER NEEDS

**THE MAN'S MOST BASIC NEEDS:**

1. Sexual fulfillment
2. Recreational companionship
3. An attractive spouse
4. Domestic support
5. Admiration

**THE WOMAN'S MOST BASIC NEEDS:**

1. Affection
2. Conversation
3. Honesty and openness
4. Financial support
5. Family commitment

*Time and again these ten needs have surfaced as I have helped literally thousands of couples improve their troubled marriages. Although each individual may perceive his or her needs differently, the consistency with which these two sets of five categories have surfaced to explain marital problems impresses me.*

WILLARD HARLEY
CONDENSED FROM "HIS NEEDS, HER NEEDS"

# SPRINGBOARDS TO DEEPER CONVERSATION

### 1.

*What is the happiest thing that has ever happened to you?*

### 2.

*What has been the hardest experience of your life?*

### 3.

*What are your secret ambitions, your goals for your life?*

### 4.

*What are your deep fears?*

### 5.

*What about me do you appreciate the most?*

### 6.

*What traits of mine would you like to see changed?*

### 7.

*What people do you most admire?*

CAROLE MAYHALL
CONDENSED FROM "LORD, TEACH ME WISDOM"

MARRIAGE

# THINGS **NOT** TO SAY TO YOUR SPOUSE

"I told you so."

"I can do whatever I like."

"You're just like your mother."

"If you don't like it, you can just leave."

"You're always in a bad mood."

"Can't you do anything right?"

"You just don't think."

"That was stupid."

"It's your fault."

"All you ever do is think of yourself."

"What's wrong with you?"

"If you really loved me, you'd do this."

"All you ever do is complain."

"You're such a baby."

"I can't do anything to please you."

"Turnabout's fair play."

"You get what you deserve."

"Why don't you ever listen to me?"

"What's your problem?"

"Can't you be more responsible?"

"I can never understand you."

"What were you thinking?"

"Do you always have to be right?"

"You're impossible!"

"I don't know why I put up with you."

"You deserve a dose of your own medicine."

DR. STEVE STEPHENS
FROM "MARRIAGE: EXPERIENCE THE BEST"

# THINGS TO SAY TO YOUR SPOUSE

"I love you."

"I was wrong."

"Good job!"

"What would you like?"

"You are wonderful."

"What is on your mind?"

"That was really great."

"Let me just listen."

"You are so special."

"I missed you today."

"What can I do to help?"

"I couldn't get you off my mind today."

"I appreciate all the things you've done for me all these years."

"Pray for me."

"I'm praying for you today."

"As always, you look good today."

"Thank you for loving me."

"I trust you."

"I can always count on you."

"Thank you for accepting me."

"You make me feel good."

"You make every day brighter."

"I prize every moment we spend together."

"I'm sorry."

"I love to see your eyes sparkle when you smile."

DR. STEVE STEPHENS
FROM "MARRIAGE: EXPERIENCE THE BEST"

MARRIAGE

# HOW TO MAKE YOUR
# MARRIAGE HEALTHY

## 1.
### COMMITMENT

*True commitment means much more than simply committing
to staying married. Genuine commitment involves being committed
to the growth and best interest of your partner.*

## 2.
### TEAMWORK

*Use the five most important words in marriage:
"Let's try it your way."*

## 3.
### COMMUNICATION

*Without exception, every couple I have ever worked with
struggles with effective communication.
Part of the reason is that two people with the exact same
communication style rarely marry each other.*

## 4.
### MEETING EMOTIONAL NEEDS

*Discover and then meet the emotional needs
of your partner. How? Simple. Just ask!*

## 5.
### RESOLVING CONFLICT

*Conflict in marriage is inevitable. Fighting is optional.*

## 6.
### APOLOGY AND FORGIVENESS

*On a regular basis, practice the three A's of successful relationships:*
*Apologize for something from the past,*
*Appreciate something in the present,*
*Anticipate something in the future.*

## 7.
### CREATING A RELATIONSHIP VISION

*Ask yourself and each other this question:*
*"If we knew we couldn't fail, and we could design our relationship*
*any way that we wanted it,*
*how would we like to be?"*

JEFF HERRING
FROM "THE OREGONIAN"

# 20 WAYS TO MAKE
# YOUR WIFE FEEL SPECIAL

1.
*Ask her to dance when you hear your love song.*

2.
*Polish her shoes for special occasions.*

3.
*Have good conversation when you'd rather read the paper.*

4.
*Give her a back rub with no expectations of lovemaking.*

5.
*Buy and plant a rose bush as a surprise.*

6.
*Keep your home repaired and in good order.*

7.
*Make sure the car has good tires and is in good running condition.*

8.
*Hold her hand when you lead the family in prayer.*

9.
*Write out a list of all your important documents and where you keep them.*

10.
*Find a way to save something from every paycheck.*

11.
*Ask her input before making decisions.*

**12.**

*Hold her tenderly when she cries and tell her it's okay.*

**13.**

*Ask her out and plan the complete date yourself—
including making the reservations.*

**14.**

*Occasionally, eat quiche and dainty desserts
with her at a Victorian restaurant.*

**15.**

*Understand when she forgets to enter a check in the ledger.*

**16.**

*Shave on your day off.*

**17.**

*Call if you're going to be more than fifteen minutes late.*

**18.**

*Encourage her to take time out with her friends.*

**19.**

*Remember to carry Kleenex or a clean handkerchief
when you go to a romantic movie.*

**20.**

*Tell her she will always be beautiful when she worries about getting older.*

AL GRAY
MARRIED 32 YEARS

MARRIAGE

# 20 WAYS TO MAKE YOUR HUSBAND FEEL SPECIAL

### 1.
*Don't interrupt or correct him when he is telling a story.*

### 2.
*Compliment him in front of his children,*
*your parents, his parents, and friends.*

### 3.
*Be as concerned about your looks as you were when you were dating.*

### 4.
*Let him have some time to relax when he first gets home.*

### 5.
*Develop a genuine interest in his work and hobbies.*

### 6.
*Admire him for his strength and significance.*

### 7.
*If he wants to take a lunch to work, pack it for him.*

### 8.
*Try to be home (and off the phone) when he gets home*
*from work, and up in the morning when he leaves.*

### 9.
*Help your kids be excited about dad coming home.*

### 10.
*Buy him new socks and underwear on ordinary days instead*
*of giving these as gifts on holidays and birthdays.*

### 11.
*Keep your bedroom tastefully decorated and clutter free.*

### 12.
*Understand when he wants to spend time
enjoying sports or hobbies with his friends.*

### 13.
*Keep his favorite snack on hand.*

### 14.
*Stick to your budget.*

### 15.
*Watch his favorite TV sporting events with him.*

### 16.
*Try to go to bed at the same time he does;
understand if he falls asleep in the recliner after a hard day.*

### 17.
*Trade babysitting with friends so you have some nights at home alone.*

### 18.
*Keep lovemaking fresh and exciting, and remember
he probably has more frequent desires than you have.*

### 19.
*Bake homemade cookies for him to take to work.*

### 20.
*Ask yourself one question every day: "What's it like being married to me?"*

ALICE GRAY
FROM HER SEMINAR "THREE TREASURES FOR EVERY MARRIAGE"

# TOGETHERNESS

When husbands focus only on their interests and wives focus only on their interests, the bonds of marriage break. Building togetherness in each of the following areas will strengthen your marriage and increase your love.

## 1.
*Emotional togetherness*—being tuned into each other's feelings.

## 2.
*Intellectual togetherness*—sharing thoughts, ideas, opinions, and beliefs.

## 3.
*Aesthetic togetherness*—enjoying the beauty and artistry of life.

## 4.
*Recreational togetherness*—having fun and excitement as a couple.

## 5.
*Work togetherness*—doing common, everyday tasks and chores as a team.

## 6.
*Crisis togetherness*—leaning on each other when times are hard.

## 7.
*Sexual togetherness*—bonding through physical closeness.

## 8.
*Spiritual togetherness*—drawing closer to God and encouraging each other's faith.

DR. STEVE STEPHENS
PSYCHOLOGIST AND SEMINAR SPEAKER

# 50 GIFTS FOR MARRIAGE

1. Start each day with a kiss. 2.. Wear your wedding ring at all times. 3. Date once a week. 4. Accept differences. 5. Be polite. 6. Be gentle. 7. Give gifts. 8. Smile often. 9. Touch. 10. Talk about dreams. 11. Choose a song that can be "your song." 12. Give back rubs. 13. Laugh together. 14. Send a card for no reason. 15. Do what your spouse wants before being asked. 16. Listen. 17. Encourage. 18. Do it the other's way. 19. Know your mate's needs. 20. Fix his (or her) favorite breakfast. 21. Compliment your partner twice a day. 22. Call just to say "I love you." 23. Slow down. 24. Hold hands. 25. Cuddle. 26. Ask your spouse's opinion. 27. Show respect. 28. Welcome each other home. 29. Look your best for your mate. 30. Wink at each other. 31. Celebrate birthdays in a big way. 32. Apologize. 33. Forgive. 34. Set up a romantic getaway. 35. Ask, "What can I do to make you happier?" 36. Be positive. 37. Be kind. 38. Be vulnerable. 39. Respond quickly to your mate's requests. 40. Talk about your love. 41. Reminisce about your favorite times together. 42. Treat his (or her) friends and relatives with courtesy. 43. Send flowers every Valentine's Day and anniversary. 44. Admit when you are wrong. 45. Be sensitive to your mate's sexual desires. 46. Pray for him (or her) daily. 47. Watch sunsets together. 48. Say "I love you" frequently. 49. End each day with a hug. 50. Seek outside help when you need it.

DR. STEVE STEPHENS
FROM "UNDERSTANDING THE ONE YOU LOVE"

# BEING A REAL MAN

### 1.
*A real man includes his wife in envisioning the future.*

### 2.
*A real man accepts spiritual responsibility for his family.*

### 3.
*A real man is willing to say "I'm sorry" and "Forgive me" to his family.*

### 4.
*A real man discusses household responsibilities with his
wife and makes sure they are fairly distributed.*

### 5.
*A real man seeks the consultation of his wife
on all major financial decisions.*

### 6.
*A real man follows through with commitments he has made to his wife.*

### 7.
*A real man frequently tells his wife what he likes about her.*

### 8.
*A real man provides financially for his family's basic living expenses.*

### 9.
*A real man deals with distractions so he
can unite with his wife and family.*

### 10.
*A real man prays with his wife on a regular basis.*

### 11.
*A real man initiates meaningful family traditions.*

**12.**

*A real man initiates family outings for the family on a regular basis.*

**13.**

*A real man takes the time to give his children practical instruction about life, which in turn gives them confidence with their peers.*

**14.**

*A real man manages the schedule of the home and anticipates any pressure points.*

**15.**

*A real man keeps his family financially sound and out of harmful debt.*

**16.**

*A real man makes sure he and his wife have drawn up a will and arranged a well-conceived plan for their children in case of death.*

**17.**

*A real man lets his wife and children into the interior of his life.*

**18.**

*A real man honors his wife often in public.*

**19.**

*A real man encourages his wife to grow as an individual.*

**20.**

*A real man provides time for his wife to pursue her own personal interests.*

DR. ROBERT LEWIS, PASTOR, FELLOWSHIP BIBLE CHURCH
LITTLE ROCK, ARKANSAS

MARRIAGE

# BONDS OF INTIMACY

*Physical touching of an affectionate, nonsexual nature*

*Shared feelings*

*Closeness without inhibitions*

*Absence of psychological defenses*

*Open communication and honesty*

*Intellectual agreement on major issues*

*Spiritual harmony*

*Sensitive appreciation of the mate's physical and emotional responses*

*Similar values held*

*Imparted secrets*

*Genuine understanding*

*Mutual confidence*

*A sense of warmth, safety, and realization when together*

*Sensuous nearness*

*Sexual pleasures lovingly shared*

*Signs of love freely given and received*

*Mutual responsibility and caring*

*Abiding trust*

ED WHEAT, M.D.
CONDENSED FROM "LOVE LIFE FOR EVERY MARRIED COUPLE"

# REIGNITING ROMANCE AFTER AGE 50

In our national survey on long-term marriage, we discovered
that sexual satisfaction actually goes up, not down, for those married
thirty-plus years. So how can you reignite the spark?

### BE AFFECTIONATE.

*Romance isn't reserved just for the bedroom. Being affectionate, thoughtful and
kind at other times will spill into your love life. Phone calls, notes, holding hands,
a peck on the cheek, a wink across the room will add romance to your relationship.*

### BE A LISTENER.

*Two of the most important lovemaking skills and romance enhancers
are listening with your heart and talking to your spouse.*

### BE ADVENTURESOME.

*Try a little spontaneity. Explore.*

### BE PLAYFUL.
*Romance depends on your attitude and perspective.*

### GET IN SHAPE.

*Get enough exercise. Eat right and get enough sleep. An annual
physical is a good investment in the health of your marriage.*

### BE A LITTLE WACKY.

*What can you do to jolt your old patterns? Plan a getaway and kidnap your wife. Or
surprise her by coming home early or by taking off a morning and staying home together.*

CLAUDIA AND DAVID ARP
FROM "NEW MAN" MAGAZINE

# 20 CREATIVE, ROMANTIC IDEAS THAT COST UNDER $20

**1.**

Dress up for a meal you bring home from your favorite fast-food restaurant. Take out a tablecloth, centerpiece, and a tape recorder of your favorite romantic music and dine to a "Golden Arches" delight.

**2.**

Buy a half gallon of your favorite ice cream, go to the most beautiful park in town, throw a blanket on the ground, and eat the whole thing.

**3.**

Visit a museum or art gallery. Talk with each other about the art you like and dislike. Use the "twenty questions" method to learn all you can about why your spouse likes or dislikes what you see. Concentrate on listening to the other person and learning all you can from what he or she says.

**4.**

Go to a driving range together. Cheer each other's good shots.

**5.**

Go bowling together. Come up with prizes you can give each other for winning games; i.e., a massage, a week's worth of doing dishes, a promise to paint the fence, etc.

**6.**

Go on a hayride with four other couples, singing camp songs from a tape recorder or guitar. Plan a cookout under the stars afterward.

**7.**

Write love notes to one another and hide them in unusual places like the freezer, a shoe, the car's glove box, the bathtub, her makeup kit, or under the bed covers.

**8.**

Go snorkeling in a lake.

**9.**

Collect leaves and pine cones together on an autumn day. Take them home and make fall ornaments for the house.

**10.**
Attend a free outdoor concert.

**11.**
Buy a pass from the Forest Service, go to a National Forest, and cut your own Christmas tree.

**12.**
Buy a modern paraphrase of the Song of Solomon and read it to one another.

**13.**
Walk hand in hand along a nature trail.

**14.**
Watch a sunset together.

**15.**
Make "dough" ornaments together, bake them, and then color them with the kids.

**16.**
Rent each other's all-time favorite movies and play a double feature at home.

**17.**
Go to your favorite restaurant for dessert. Bring a child's baby book or your wedding album and relive some memories together.

**18.**
Throw a party commemorating your spouse's graduation date.

**19.**
Get the children together and make a "Why I Love Mom" and "Why I Love Dad" book, complete with text and illustrations.

**20.**
Take your spouse out for an afternoon in her favorite store. Note the items under twenty dollars she likes best. Return to the store the next day and buy one of these items as a gift.

GARY SMALLEY WITH JOHN TRENT
FROM "LOVE IS A DECISION"

MARRIAGE

# 10 SUGGESTIONS FOR TOUCHING

### 1.

Show each other where you like to be touched and the kind of touch that pleases you. Usually, a light touch is the most thrilling. Be imaginative in the way you caress.

### 2.

Demonstrate to each other how you prefer to be held. Kiss your partner the way you would like to be kissed—not to criticize past performances, but to communicate something your partner has not sensed before.

### 3.

To learn the art of expressing warm, sensual feelings, you will have to slow down. If what you are doing feels good, take the time to enjoy it.

### 4.

Caress each other's back. Pay special attention to the back of the neck at the hairline and the area just above the small of the back.

### 5.

Make sure that both of you are having equal opportunity to give and to receive. Take turns giving pleasure to each other.

### 6.

Have a period of fifteen to thirty minutes every night to lie in each other's arms in the dark before you drift off to sleep. Whisper together, sharing private thoughts and pleasant little experiences of the day. This is the time to build intimacy and wind down for sleep.

### 7.

Establish the cozy habit of staying in some sort of physical contact while you are going to sleep—a hand or a leg touching your partner's, for instance.

### 8.

Begin every day with a few minutes of cuddling and snuggling before you get out of bed. A husband can tell his wife how nice she feels and how glad he is to be close to her. A wife can nestle in her husband's arms and tell him she wishes they didn't have to leave each other that morning. Just be close and savor gentle physical contact for awhile.

### 9.

Hold hands often. Think of all the different ways you can enjoy just touching with your hands and all the different feelings that can be conveyed.

### 10.

Become aware of the many ways you can have physical contact in the course of a week. Touch when you are talking and maintain eye contact. Sit close to each other in church. Kiss each other when there is no occasion for it. Add variety to your kisses, your touches, and your love pats.

ED WHEAT, M.D.
CONDENSED FROM "LOVE LIFE FOR EVERY MARRIED COUPLE"

# WEDDING ANNIVERSARY GIFTS

| | | | | |
|---|---|---|---|---|
| 1st | Paper or clocks | 13th | Lace or textiles |
| 2nd | Cotton or china | 14th | Ivory or gold jewelry |
| 3rd | Leather or glass | 15th | Crystal or watches |
| 4th | Flowers or small appliances | 20th | China or platinum |
| 5th | Wood or silverware | 25th | Silver |
| 6th | Iron or candy | 30th | Pearl |
| 7th | Wool or copper | 35th | Coral or jade |
| 8th | Bronze or linen | 40th | Ruby |
| 9th | Pottery or leather | 45th | Sapphire |
| 10th | Aluminum or diamond | 50th | Gold |
| 11th | Steel or jewelry | 55th | Emerald |
| 12th | Silk or pearls | 60th | Diamond |

SELECTED

# HOME
*Where life gets organized*

6

# ORGANIZING MAIL

HANDLE EACH PIECE OF MAIL ONLY ONCE BY PRACTICING THE FOUR D'S:

Do it now *(pay the bill, answer the letter).*

Delegate *(pass on for someone else to handle).*

Delay it *(put it in project file to deal with).*

Dump it *(into the trash can).*

AUTHOR UNKNOWN

# OVERCOMING CLUTTER

### 1.
#### MINIMIZE YOUR BELONGINGS.

Every few months go through clothes, toys, books, games, and even furnishings. Give away things you don't use.

### 2.
#### CAREFULLY CONSIDER YOUR PURCHASES.

The more you have, the more time, space, and energy is required from you to maintain those purchases. Whenever you purchase something new, discard an old item.

### 3.
#### CREATE A RECYCLE CENTER.

You can purchase a variety of systems or create your own. Locate an easily accessible space to put paper sacks—one sack for each type of recyclable material.

### 4.
#### GO THROUGH YOUR MAIL RIGHT AWAY.

Use an accordion file folder labeled with your various household bills. Include a "To Be Paid" section. When you pay your bills move receipts to correct category. Include a "Tax Info" section to file tax information and receipts.

### 5.
#### RECYCLE JUNK MAIL.

Don't waste time opening it. Tear or shred credit card opportunities to avoid theft. Request that catalog companies not sell or rent your name.

### 6.
#### RECYCLE MAGAZINES.

If you are saving magazines because of good articles, file the articles in a three-ring notebook by category and recycle the magazines.

### 7.
#### ORGANIZE CHILDREN'S SCHOOLWORK.

Purchase large three-ring notebooks with a clear cover and spine. Let each child design their own notebook. Include grade level, school year, and other pertinent information. Divide the notebook by subjects.

### 8.
#### CREATE AN "INFORMATION CENTER."

Install some cork on the inside of one of your upper kitchen cabinets to keep all your "notes and loose paper" information.

### 9.
#### IMPLEMENT "THE BOX."

Find a box that will fit in a closet or some other enclosed space. At the end of each day collect items your family chooses to leave lying around and put them in "The Box." Items can be earned back by doing extra chores. If they are not redeemed within a week, the items are yours to do with as you please.

### 10.
#### GIVE TO CHARITY.

What is extra or unused might be needed by someone else. Teach children to give away extra toys. Let them choose the charity and go with you to drop them off.

ALLISON ALLISON
INTERIOR DESIGNER

# HINTS FOR
# KITCHEN ORGANIZATION

### 1.

Do not store cookies, cereal, or other "bait" by the stove. Children can get burned climbing on the stove to reach an item overhead.

### 2.

Use glass or ceramic pans for baking; you can reduce your oven temperature by twenty-five degrees.

### 3.

I've found an easy way to clean the cheese grater: before using it, spray it with no-stick vegetable spray.

### 4.

Put a decorative hook by the sink. Hang your watch and rings on it while you work.

### 5.

Glue a twelve-inch square of cork to the inside of the cabinet door over your kitchen work area. On the cork tack the recipe card you are using and newspaper clippings of recipes you plan to try within a few days. It keeps them at eye level and they stay spatter-free.

## 6.

Increase your efficiency with an extra-long phone cord or a cordless phone, to reach to all corners of your kitchen. Instead of wasting time while on the phone, you can cook, set the table, or clean out a drawer.

## 7.

Meat slices easier if it's partially frozen.

## 8.

Want to mix frozen juice in a hurry without using the blender? Use your potato masher on the concentrate.

## 9.

You can peel garlic cloves faster if you mash them lightly with the side of the blade of a chef's knife.

## 10.

To keep bugs out of your flour canister, put a stick of spearmint gum in the flour, and it will be bug-free.

EMILIE BARNES
CONDENSED FROM "MORE HOURS IN MY DAY"

# HOW LONG TO KEEP IT

Bank statements and canceled checks: Six years*

Birth or adoption certificates: Forever

Contracts: Until updated

Credit card account numbers: Until updated

Marriage or divorce papers: Forever

Home purchase and improvement records:

Even with new tax law, keep until you sell

Life insurance policies: Forever

Car, home insurance: Until updated

Investment records: Six years after tax deadline for year of sale

Loan agreements: Until updated

*Military service records: Forever*

*Real estate deeds: As long as you own property*

*Receipts for large purchases: Until sale or discard*

*Service contracts and warranties: Until sale or discard*

*Social Security card: Forever*

*Tax returns: Forever*

*Vehicle titles: Until sale or disposal*

*Will: Until updated*

*The IRS may audit returns up to three years after filing. But it has six years to challenge a return if it thinks gross income was underreported by at least 25 percent. No time limit applies to fraudulent returns.

EXCERPTED FROM "YOUR FINANCIAL ORGANIZER"
TEACHERS INSURANCE & ANNUITY ASSOCIATION

# TIME MAKERS

CONTROL PHONE USAGE.

*Limit phone conversations to fifteen minutes or less. Turn the ringer off your phone once in a while. If you have a message recorder, return calls at your convenience.*

PLAN FOR CHILDREN'S BOREDOM.

*Make space in a cupboard and fill it with prepared activities.*

DO MAJOR GROCERY SHOPPING AT ONE STORE.

*It saves time and energy that may be better used somewhere else.*

PREPARE GROCERY LIST AHEAD OF TIME.

*Organize your list by store aisles, including brand names you prefer.*

COOK MEALS IN BULK.

*Double recipes and freeze half to use later.*

SCHEDULE YOUR TASKS.

*Do routine tasks, such as laundry, on a specific day of the week.*

### DESIGNATE A BILL DAY.

*Pay bills at the same time each month to avoid missing due dates. If you don't have the money to pay all your bills at once, do this twice a month.*

### MAKE A "REFERENCE BINDER."

*Create a three-ring "reference binder" with takeout menus, phone lists, birthdays, emergency information and whatever else you frequently need.*

### ENJOY YOUR LIFE.

*With the extra time you've saved, visit a friend, take a walk, read a good book, or just relax.*

ALLISON ALLISON
INTERIOR DESIGNER

# BABYSITTER CHECKLIST

*Write out instructions for all of the following information:*

### Emergency Information

✓ Emergency phone numbers for police, fire, and poison control
✓ Street address and phone number at residence
✓ Nearest cross streets
✓ Parent(s) names
✓ Where to reach parent(s)
✓ Phone numbers of available neighbors
✓ Instructions regarding medications and allergies
✓ Location of first aid kit
✓ Fire escape route

### General Information

✓ Names and ages of children
✓ Feeding routines
✓ Bedtime routines
✓ Discipline preferences
✓ Guidelines for television, computer, telephone, food
✓ Visitor restrictions for children and sitter
✓ Expectations for kitchen cleanup or other chores
  for children and sitter

ALICE GRAY
SEMINAR SPEAKER

# FOUR AXIOMS OF SPENDING

## 1
*The more shopping we do,*
*the more we spend.*

## 2
*The more we watch television,*
*the more we spend.*

## 3
*The more time we spend looking*
*through catalogs, the more we spend.*

## 4
*The more we read magazines and newspaper*
*advertisements, the more we spend.*

HOWARD L. DAYTON, JR.
FROM "GETTING OUT OF DEBT POCKET GUIDE"™

# SIMPLE WAYS TO CUT EXPENSES

### 1.

USE A FIFTEEN-YEAR INSTEAD OF A THIRTY-YEAR
MORTGAGE ON YOUR HOME.

### 2.

REFINANCE YOUR MORTGAGE.

*If interest rates have dropped substantially, check with your bank or
mortgage company about the cost of refinancing.*

### 3.

SET YOUR THERMOSTAT FIVE DEGREES WARMER IN THE SUMMER
AND FIVE DEGREES COOLER IN THE WINTER.

*Your utility savings will be dramatic.*

### 4.

KEEP DRIVING THE CAR YOU HAVE
INSTEAD OF PURCHASING A NEW ONE.

*Ron Blue says it best when he observes, "The cheapest
car to own is the one you are driving."*

### 5.

USE A SELF-SERVICE INSTEAD OF FULL-SERVICE GAS STATION, IF POSSIBLE.

*The savings can result in several hundred dollars a year. The only
item you really need to check once a week is the oil.*

## 6.

REFUSE TO SHOP FOR GROCERIES WHEN YOU ARE HUNGRY.

*Waiting until after you have eaten can prevent wasteful spending.*

## 7.

USE A LIST WHEN YOU SHOP FOR GROCERIES.

*Impulse buying can destroy your food budget.*

## 8.

POSTPONE CLOTHES PURCHASES UNTIL MAJOR SALES.

*You will be amazed at how much money you can save.*

## 9.

SPLIT ENTREES WHEN YOU EAT OUT.

*Most restaurants serve more food than you'll ever want to eat.*

## 10.

PLAN YOUR TRAVEL AHEAD OF TIME.

*Airlines and hotels penalize those who make last-minute travel plans.*

ROBERT JEFFRESS
CONDENSED FROM "SAY GOODBYE TO REGRET"

# PLANNING AHEAD FOR HOLIDAY SHOPPING

### *Shopping Lists*

- Make a list of everyone receiving gifts.
- Determine total budget for Christmas shopping.
- Try to spend less than the previous year.
- Decide early what gifts you will make.
- Figure out the maximum you will spend on each person.
- Record favorite colors and correct sizes.
- Write down ideas you come across during the year.
- Keep current with kids' fads and trends.
- Choose a ministry or needy family and include some outreach gifts.
- Never go shopping without your list.

### *Shopping Days*

- Order from catalogs and mail directly to recipient's home.
- Don't wait until Thanksgiving weekend to begin shopping.
- Finish by December 15.
- Avoid carrying a big purse, heavy coat, or umbrella.
- Use a small purse with strap that crosses over your shoulder to free hands.

- Only take checkbook, cash, credit cards, I.D., Kleenex, car keys, shopping list, paper, and pencil.
- Trade babysitting with a friend and leave the children at home.
- If children go with you, shorten your shopping time.
- Ask for gift boxes or use free wrapping service when provided.
- Enjoy a treat from the espresso or juice bar.
- Don't forget where you parked the car.
- Take time to enjoy the lights, the people, and *the season*.

### *After Shopping*

- Make a wrapping center at home and wrap gifts as you buy.
- Consider enclosing receipts for easy returns.
- Keep all other receipts in a separate envelope.
- Mail out-of-town gifts early.
- When family or friends visit, send packages home with them.
- Light a fragrant candle and play Christmas music.
- Enjoy the *Reason for the season*.

BECKY MCCLURE
SEMINAR SPEAKER

# HOLIDAY ENTERTAINING
# WITH LESS STRESS

### Food Preparation

- Write out complete menus in advance.
- Select simple menus and use the same menu more than once.
- Bake cookies, breads, and rolls in advance and keep in the freezer.
- Make frozen salads and desserts in advance.
- Include other family members in the planning and responsibilities.
- Make out a list and purchase all nonperishable items at one time.
- Purchase perishable items weekly.
- Every night look over your calendar and make a list for the next day.

### Home Preparation

- Clean your house thoroughly the first week in December.
- Spot clean your house weekly.
- Put up outside lights the first week in December.
- Decorate inside your house (except for the tree) the first week in December.
- Use artificial greens so they will not need to be replaced.
- Put up and decorate your tree the second week in December.

### *Time Out for Your Family*

- Plan some family nights.
- Drive to see the Christmas lights.
- Attend a musical or play.
- Gather around the tree and roast marshmallows in the fireplace.
- Entertain with less stress and greater pleasure.
- Keep a candle burning and enjoy the fragrance...but don't burn your candle at both ends.

BECKY MCCLURE
SEMINAR SPEAKER

# MAKE YOUR OLD HOME
## FEEL LIKE NEW

### 1.

*See the potential.* Look beyond the chipped paint and the worn and cracked linoleum to the charm of the architecture and don't be afraid of what it will take to make this "find" your dream home.

### 2.

*First room to redecorate.* Decide which room you will spend a lot of time in.

### 3.

*Complete one room at a time.* This will encourage you to keep going. You will be better able to see results when an entire room is redone than if you do one or two small things in several rooms. This can be discouraging.

### 4.

*Paint.* The cheapest way to decorate is with paint. It is amazing how a couple coats of paint will transform the drabbest of rooms. Paint the walls a different shade than the woodwork if you have painted woodwork.

### 5.

*Wallpaper.* My absolute favorite way to decorate is with wallpaper. Pick high-quality paper; though it is more costly, it will last for years. Try papering the top half of the room with a border, or perhaps just one wall in the room (this will cut costs). Rooms that are papered need fewer decorative items on the walls as your wallpaper is part of the decorating. *Nothing* transforms a room like wallpaper.

## 6.

*Big budget items.* Carpet, linoleum, counter tops, etc. Tackle these items as your budget allows. Paint and wallpaper will transform enough of your house until you can afford to replace the more costly items.

## 7.

*Color.* Pick two or three main colors and use these same colors and their various shades to decorate the entire house. Too many colors make a house look chopped up; you want your house to "flow" from room to room. You don't have to use only these three colors in every room—you can add one or two accent colors with your three primary colors.

## 8.

*Decorating ideas.* If you are at a loss as to how to decorate your home, decorating magazines and wallpaper books are full of great ideas. Visit some model homes as well.

## 9.

*Most of all, have fun* making your home your own personal "haven."

NANCY LARSON
HOME MAKEOVER CONSULTANT TO FRIENDS

# HOME SAFETY TIPS

1.

*Keep stairs and surrounding areas well-lit,
unobstructed, and in good repair.*

2.

*Use nonslip mats in the tub and on the bathroom floor,
along with wall-mounted grab bars, to help prevent falls.*

3.

*Keep household chemicals and medicines locked up.
Some common products containing alcohol, such as
mouthwash, can be harmful to children.*

4.

*Test smoke detectors once each month,
and change batteries every six months.*

5.

*Sleep with bedroom doors closed to keep toxic gases out in case of fire.*

6.

*Douse smoking materials with water before discarding.*

## 7.
*Install a carbon monoxide detector to monitor
furnaces, dryers, and space heaters.*

## 8.
*Make it a rule to never leave a child unattended at a pool.*

## 9.
*Install fencing with self-closing and self-latching gates around pools.*

## 10.
*Remember that small children can fall into
toilets, even five-gallon buckets, and drown.*

## 11.
*Make your kitchen "off-limits" to children while you are cooking.*

## 12.
*Install anti-scalding devices on tubs and showers.*

## 13.
*Use ground-fault circuit interrupters in outlets near water to prevent shocks.*

TOM PHILBIN, FROM "PARADE" MAGAZINE
REPRINTED WITH PERMISSION FROM "PARADE MAGAZINE" © 1988

# CRIME STOPPERS' CHECKLIST

✔ *Do you have a dog?* Barking dogs attract the kind of attention a burglar doesn't need.

✔ *Do you leave a radio or television set on when you're out?* The sound of voices will send an intruder elsewhere.

✔ *Do you refuse to open doors to strangers?* Always ask for identification or check the driveway for a repair or delivery truck. If in doubt, call the utility or business in question to ask if they have sent someone to your home.

✔ *Do you have peepholes in all solid doors?* Don't rely on chain locks to see who is at the door. They can easily be forced once a door is ajar.

✔ *Do you keep your garage door locked?* Thieves like attached garages because, once inside, they can unobtrusively force the door to the house.

✔ *Are your basement windows secure?* These are another popular point of entry for intruders.

✔ *Do you keep trees and shrubbery trimmed?* Overgrown vegetation gives a burglar more privacy.

✔ *Do you have neighbors collect your mail and newspapers while you're away?* You can also ask the post office and paper carrier to hold deliveries until you return.

✔ *Have you familiarized babysitters and other outsiders with your safety measures?* Show them escape routes and familiarize them with any locks and alarm systems.

✔ *Does your neighborhood have a watch program?* If not, check with your local police for information about starting one.

SELECTED FROM 'ABOUT...KEEPING YOUR HOME SAFE,' A LIFE ADVICE® PAMPHLET
PUBLISHED BY METLIFE'S CONSUMER EDUCATION CENTER

# FIRE SAFETY CHECKLIST

✓ *Are your smoke detectors working?* There should be at least one on every floor of your home. Test each detector monthly and replace batteries annually.

✓ *Do you hold regular fire drills?* Several times a year, have your family practice exiting your home safely and quickly in the event of an emergency. Designate a meeting place for all family members to gather once they are out of the house.

✓ *Have you taught your children to "stop, drop and roll"?* In the event their clothing catches fire, kids (and adults) should stop, drop to the floor, cover their faces, and roll over and over or back and forth to put out the fire. Keep rolling until the fire goes out.

✓ *Have you planned an alternate escape route?* It's important to have at least two escape routes from each room in your home, often a door and a window. Practice using them now to be sure you could get out in an emergency.

✓ *Can you safely exit from the second floor?* A chain ladder or other easily accessible ladder can help you escape from the upper stories of your home in the event of a fire.

✓ *Do you know how to use your fire extinguishers?* Know where your fire extinguishers are kept, and read the instructions for use before you need them.

✓ *Do you know the phone number for your local fire department and the location of the nearest phone outside your house?* In case of fire, always evacuate your home first, then call for help from a cellular or other nearby phone.

SELECTED FROM "ABOUT...KEEPING YOUR HOME SAFE," A LIFE ADVICE® PAMPHLET
PUBLISHED BY METLIFE'S CONSUMER EDUCATION CENTER

# PREPARE FOR DISASTERS

### 1.

Discuss the disasters most likely to happen in your area and their impact on your family's safety. Hazards include home fires, harsh winter weather, earthquakes, flooding, and hazardous materials threats.

### 2.

Train all family members. Enroll all members of your household in first aid classes. Learn to use a fire extinguisher and how to shut off utilities. Don't take a chance that the only person who knows first aid or how to turn off the natural gas will be at home when needed. Learn how to respond safely to earthquakes and other disasters.

### 3.

Assemble emergency supplies including food, water, a flashlight, a battery-powered radio, extra batteries, a first aid kit, extra prescription medications, and emergency tools. Store enough supplies to last your family at least three days following a disaster.

### 4.

Identify emergency names and numbers. Choose an out-of-state friend or relative to be your emergency contact. Give this person's name and number to all members of your household so when local phones are down, they can use their out-of-state contact to relay messages to one another.

### 5.

Maintain your readiness. Review your plan at least once a year to determine what training, equipment, and supplies are needed. Commit to a day or weekend to update phone numbers, hold fire and earthquake drills, and check supplies.

FROM THE AMERICAN RED CROSS
OREGON TRAIL CHAPTER

# HEALTH

*A long and satisfying life*

7

# DANGER SIGNALS OF STRESS

YOU MAY BE UNDER TOO MUCH STRESS IF YOU...

*...find yourself irritable or impatient with things you normally tolerate.*

*...have difficulty getting to sleep and feel exhausted when you awake.*

*...sense you are one step away from falling apart.*

*...suffer from frequent headaches or stomach pains.*

*...get distracted easily and have trouble concentrating.*

*...talk more negatively than usual.*

*...become forgetful and absentminded.*

*...don't laugh as much as you used to.*

*...use alcohol, non-prescription drugs, or food to help you relax.*

*...postpone what is truly important, to accomplish what isn't that important.*

CAROL CLIFTON, PH.D.
LICENSED PSYCHOLOGIST

# 21 FACTORS FOR A LONG, HEALTHY LIFE

## IN ORDER OF IMPORTANCE:

### 1.
*Not smoking.*

### 2.
*Not smoking in bed, if you do smoke.*

### 3.
*Wearing your seat belt.*

### 4.
*Not drinking and driving*

### 5.
*Having a smoke detector in your home.*

### 6.
*Socializing regularly.*

### 7.
*Getting frequent strenuous exercise.*

### 8.
*Drinking alcohol moderately.* *

### 9.
*Avoiding home accidents.*

### 10.
*Limiting fat in your diet.*

### 11.
*Maintaining your proper weight.*

### 12.
*Obeying the speed limit.*

*EDITORIAL COMMENT...IF AT ALL

13.
*Getting an annual blood pressure test.*

14.
*Controlling stress.*

15.
*Consuming fiber.*

16.
*Limiting cholesterol in your diet.*

17.
*Getting adequate vitamins and minerals.*

18.
*Having an annual dental exam.*

19.
*Limiting sodium in your diet.*

20.
*Limiting consumption of sugar and sweets.*

21.
*Getting seven to eight hours sleep each night.*

FROM THE "PREVENTION INDEX"

# DO YOU NEED MORE SLEEP?

TAKE THE FOLLOWING TRUE/FALSE QUIZ AND SEE FOR YOURSELF.

### 1.
*I need an alarm clock to wake up at the appropriate time.*

### 2.
*It's a struggle for me to get out of bed in the morning.*

### 3.
*Weekday mornings I hit the snooze button several
times to get more sleep.*

### 4.
*I feel tired, irritable, and stressed-out during the week.*

### 5.
*I have trouble concentrating and remembering.*

### 6.
*I feel slow in critical thinking, problem solving, and being creative.*

### 7.
*I often fall asleep watching TV.*

### 8.
*I often fall asleep in meetings, in lectures, or in warm rooms.*

### 9.
*I often fall asleep after heavy meals or after a low dose of alcohol.*

**10.**

*I often fall asleep while relaxing after dinner.*

**11.**

*I often fall asleep within five minutes of getting into bed.*

**12.**

*I often feel drowsy while driving.*

**13.**

*I often sleep extra hours on weekend mornings.*

**14.**

*I often need a nap to get through the day.*

**15.**

*I have dark circles around my eyes.*

IF YOU ANSWERED "TRUE" TO THREE OR MORE OF THE
FIFTEEN ITEMS, YOU PROBABLY ARE NOT GETTING ENOUGH SLEEP.
UNFORTUNATELY, YOU ARE NOT ALONE.

PATRICIA ANSTETT
FROM "THE OREGONIAN"

# SEVEN WAYS TO KEEP YOUR BRAIN CELLS WORKING

### 1.

*Play complex puzzles and games such as Scrabble or chess.*

### 2.

*Learn a foreign language.*

### 3.

*Study music.*

### 4.

*Solve math problems without using a calculator.*

### 5.

*Write letters or poetry.*

### 6.

*Engage in thought-provoking discussions.*

### 7.

*Study and memorize Scripture.*

AUTHOR UNKNOWN

# KEYS TO A LIFETIME OF FITNESS

TIPS TO MAKE EXERCISE A HABIT

*Choose an activity you enjoy.*

*Tailor your program to your own fitness level.*

*Set realistic goals.*

*Choose an exercise that fits your lifestyle.*

*Give your body a chance to adjust to your new routine.*

*Don't get discouraged if you don't see immediate results.*

*Don't give up if you miss a day; just get back on track the next day.*

*Find a partner for a little motivation and socialization.*

*Build some rest days into your exercise schedule.*

*Listen to your body. If you have difficulty breathing or*

*experience faintness or prolonged weakness*

*during or after exercise, consult your physician.*

CONDENSED FROM "ABOUT...FITNESS AND EXERCISE," A LIFE ADVICE® PAMPHLET
PUBLISHED BY METLIFE'S CONSUMER EDUCATION CENTER

HEALTH

# BENEFITS OF EXERCISE

### IMPROVED HEALTH

*Increased efficiency of heart and lungs*
*Reduced cholesterol levels*
*Increased muscle strength*
*Reduced blood pressure*
*Reduced risk of major illnesses*
*such as diabetes and heart disease*
*Weight loss*

### IMPROVED SENSE OF WELL-BEING

*More energy*
*Less stress*
*Improved quality of sleep*
*Improved ability to cope with stress*
*Increased mental acuity*

### IMPROVED APPEARANCE

*Weight loss*
*Toned muscles*
*Improved posture*

## ENHANCED SOCIAL LIFE

*Improved self-image*
*Increased opportunities to make new friends*
*Increased opportunities to share an*
*activity with friends or family members*


## INCREASED STAMINA

*Increased productivity*
*Increased physical capabilities*
*Less frequent injuries*
*Improved immunity to minor illnesses*

CONDENSED FROM "ABOUT...FITNESS AND EXERCISE," A LIFE ADVICE® PAMPHLET
PUBLISHED BY METLIFE'S CONSUMER EDUCATION CENTER

# 10 SIMPLE WAYS TO BUILD EXERCISE INTO YOUR DAY

### 1.

Use the stairs instead of the elevator. Set a rule for yourself that any time you are going up or down fewer than five floors, you take the stairs.

### 2.

If you take the bus, train, or subway to work or school, don't board it at the closest stop to your home. Instead, make it a habit to walk to a stop twenty to thirty minutes away.

### 3.

If it is practical, ride your bike to work instead of taking a car or other transportation. If this is not practical, ride your bike or walk on errands or when going to the market.

### 4.

Take an exercise break instead of a coffee break. Keep a pair of tennis shoes at your office and walk around the block a couple of times.

### 5.

Leave your car parked at the farthest end of a parking lot and walk vigorously to your destination. Walk completely around a mall before you start shopping.

### 6.

While at home watching television, ride an exercise bike or use a rowing machine. If you don't have either, do ten situps during every commercial break of any one-hour program you watch. Build up to twenty situps, then thirty, and finally fifty.

### 7.

While doing simple chores around the home, wear ankle and wrist weights.

### 8.

Next time you have to drive the kids to work, band practice, or Little League, walk them there instead.

### 9.

Perhaps there is no way you can find fifty minutes a day for regular exercise, so do the next best thing. Find five ten-minute intervals throughout the day to get your exercising done.

### 10.

Set your alarm fifteen minutes early each day and take a short walk to a special place near your home.

CARL DREIZLER AND MARY E. EHEMANN
FROM "52 WAYS TO LOSE WEIGHT"

# BACK SAVERS

---

*Bend at your hips, not at your waist.*

*Avoid lying on your stomach.*

*Lift heavy objects no higher than your waist.*

*Sit down to put on socks, shoes, pants—don't bend over.*

*Get down on one knee before picking up
a small child or infant from the floor.*

*When reading, don't bend your neck and shoulders—bring
your book up to your eyes by placing two pillows on your lap
and propping the book on top of them.*

FROM "THE BACK ALMANAC"

---

# 12 REASONS TO KEEP YOUR CHILD HOME FROM SCHOOL

1.
*A high temperature*

2.
*Lice or scabies (until treated)*

3.
*A cold with a fever*

4.
*A sore throat with fever*

5.
*An earache or headache*

6.
*Diarrhea and/or abdominal cramps*

7.
*Nausea and/or vomiting*

8.
*Any skin injury or burn that may become infected*

9.
*Any infectious disease*

10.
*Conjunctivitis (pinkeye)*

11.
*Your own judgment that your child isn't well*

12.
*Your child is overly tired*

PAT VAN DIEST
REGISTERED NURSE

HEALTH

# 10 WAYS TO HELP PREVENT HEART DISEASE

### 1.

*Know your risk factors (high cholesterol, bad diet, smoking, obesity, lack of exercise, other diseases such as diabetes and hypertension).*

### 2.

*Ask your doctor about taking an aspirin a day.*

### 3.

*Have regular medical checkups.*

### 4.

*Get your blood pressure and cholesterol under control.*

### 5.

*Replace a bad habit such as smoking with a good one like swimming.*

6.

*Eat five servings of fruit
and vegetables a day.*

7.

*Cut the fat.*

8.

*Eat fiber and whole grains.*

9.

*Walk and swim.*

10.

*Slow down.*

TERRY SHINTANI AND J.M.T. MILLER
FROM "52 WAYS TO PREVENT HEART DISEASE"

HEALTH

# RECOGNIZE A HEART ATTACK!

When a heart attack occurs, there's no time for delay.
The symptoms of a heart attack vary, but the usual warning signs are:

### 1.
*Uncomfortable pressure, fullness, squeezing, or pain in the center of
the chest lasting more than a few minutes.*

### 2.
*Pain spreading to the shoulders, neck, or arms.*

### 3.
*Chest discomfort with lightheadedness, fainting, sweating,
nausea, or shortness of breath.*

Not all of these signs occur in every attack. In some cases, the symptoms
subside and then return. If you notice one or more of these signs, don't wait.
Get medical help right away!

AMERICAN HEART ASSOCIATION

# RECOGNIZE A STROKE!

### 1.
*Sudden weakness or numbness of the face,
arm, or leg on one side of the body.*

### 2.
*Sudden dimness or loss of vision, particularly in one eye.*

### 3.
*Loss of speech or trouble talking or understanding speech.*

### 4.
*Sudden, severe headaches with no apparent cause.*

### 5.
*Unexplained dizziness, unsteadiness, or sudden falls, especially
along with any of the previous symptoms.*

YOU ARE PARTICULARLY AT RISK FOR STROKE IF YOU HAVE:

### 1.
*Diagnosed high blood pressure.*

### 2.
*Diagnosed heart disease.*

The warning signs listed above may be temporary, lasting anywhere from a few minutes to almost twenty-four hours. If any of these symptoms occur, get medical help right away!

AMERICAN HEART ASSOCIATION

# 14 WARNING SIGNS FOR CANCER

## KEY WARNING SIGNS

### 1.
*Change in bowel or bladder habits*

### 2.
*A sore that does not heal*

### 3.
*Unusual bleeding or discharge*

### 4.
*Thickening or lump in the breast or elsewhere*

### 5.
*Indigestion or difficulty swallowing*

### 6.
*Obvious change in a wart or mole*

### 7.
*Nagging cough or hoarseness*

## SECONDARY WARNING SIGNS

### 8.
*Chronic fatigue*

### 9.
*Prolonged depression*

### 10.
*Sudden loss of appetite*

### 11.
*Unexplained and chronic pain*

### 12.
*Any other unusual and troublesome changes in your body*

### 13.
*Long-term paleness*

### 14.
*Unexplained bruising*

THE AMERICAN CANCER SOCIETY

# WHAT CANCER CANNOT DO

CANCER IS LIMITED—

*It cannot cripple love*

*It cannot shatter hope*

*It cannot corrode faith*

*It cannot destroy peace*

*It cannot kill friendship*

*It cannot suppress memories*

*It cannot silence courage*

*It cannot invade the soul*

*It cannot steal eternal life*

*It cannot conquer the spirit.*

AUTHOR UNKNOWN

# CONTENTMENT

*Finding peace and fulfillment*

8

# A BETTER LIFE

*Feel positive emotions*

*Think positive thoughts*

*Focus on the positive in people*

*Offer positive prayers*

*Speak positive words*

*Practice positive actions*

RON JENSON
FROM "TAKING THE LEAD"

# CHOICES

*If you want to be rich...GIVE!*

*If you want to be poor...GRASP!*

*If you want abundance...SCATTER!*

*If you want to be needy...HOARD!*

JOHN LAWRENCE
FROM "THE SEVEN LAWS OF THE HARVEST"

# THE MYSTERY OF ANSWERED PRAYER

*I asked God for strength, that I might achieve;*

*I was made weak, that I might learn humbly to obey.*

*I asked for health, that I might do greater things;*

*I was given infirmity, that I might do better things.*

*I asked for riches, that I might be happy;*

*I was given poverty, that I might be wise.*

*I asked for power, that I might have the praise of men;*

*I was given weakness, that I might feel the need of God.*

*I asked for all things that I might enjoy life;*

*I was given life, that I might enjoy all things.*

*I got nothing I asked for but everything I had hoped for.*

*Almost despite myself, my unspoken prayers were answered.*

*I am, among men, most richly blessed.*

AT THE END OF THE CIVIL WAR, THIS PRAYER WAS FOUND FOLDED
IN THE POCKET OF A CONFEDERATE SOLDIER

# NINE ESSENTIALS FOR CONTENTED LIVING

1.
*Health enough to make work a pleasure*

2.
*Wealth enough to support your needs*

3.
*Strength enough to battle difficulties and overcome them*

4.
*Grace enough to confess your sins and forsake them*

5.
*Patience enough to toil until some good is accomplished*

6.
*Clarity enough to see some good in your neighbor*

7.
*Love enough to move you to be useful and helpful to others*

8.
*Faith enough to make real the things of God*

9.
*Hope enough to remove all anxious fears confronting the future*

GOETHE
POET, PLAYRIGHT, AND NOVELIST

# A PRAYER OF MOTHER TERESA

DELIVER ME...

*From the desire of being loved,*

*From the desire of being extolled,*

*From the desire of being honored,*

*From the desire of being praised,*

*From the desire of being preferred,*

*From the desire of being consulted,*

*From the desire of being approved,*

*From the desire of being popular,*

*From the fear of being humiliated,*

*From the fear of being despised,*

*From the fear of suffering rebukes,*

*From the fear of being calumniated,*

*From the fear of being forgotten,*

*From the fear of being wronged,*

*From the fear of being ridiculed,*

*From the fear of being suspected.*

LUCINDA VARDEY, ED.
FROM "MOTHER TERESA: A SIMPLE PATH"

# LEAVE IT TO GOD

Can't seem to get where you want to go fast enough?
*Leave it to God.*

Worried about the kids?
*Leave it to God.*

Living in a place you'd rather not be?
*Leave it to God.*

Looks like you won't graduate with honors?
*Leave it to God.*

No matter how hard you try, your
life's partner simply is not responding?
*Leave it to God.*

Found a lump and you see the doctor tomorrow?
*Leave it to God.*

You've said the right words to that friend
who is lost, and you've been all you know to be?
*Leave it to God.*

Haven't got a date for the prom?
*Leave it to God.*

A midcareer change seems scary?
*Leave it to God.*

You did a job, and someone else got the credit?
*Leave it to God.*

Getting older, alone?
*Leave it to God.*

CHARLES R. SWINDOLL
FROM "THE FINISHING TOUCH"

# 13 RULES TO LIVE BY

1.
*It ain't as bad as you think; it will look better in the morning.*

2.
*Get mad, then get over it.*

3.
*Avoid having your ego so close to your position that
when your position falls, your ego goes with it.*

4.
*It can be done!*

5.
*Be careful what you choose. You may get it.*

6.
*Don't let adverse facts stand in the way of a good decision.*

7.
*Check small things.*

8.
*Share credit.*

9.
*You can't make someone else's choices. You shouldn't let someone else make yours.*

10.
*Remain calm. Be kind.*

11.
*Have a vision. Be demanding.*

12.
*Don't take counsel of your fears or naysayers.*

13.
*Perpetual optimism is a force multiplier. (In the military, one is always
looking for methods of increasing or multiplying one's forces.)*

GENERAL COLIN POWELL
FROM "PARADE" MAGAZINE

# DAY BY DAY

*On this day…*
I will try to be happy. My happiness is a direct result of my being at peace
with myself; what others do or think will not determine my happiness.

*On this day…*
I will accept myself and live to the best of my ability.

*On this day…*
I will make time to pray and meditate on the Scriptures, seeking
God and developing my relationship with Him.

*On this day…*
I will say what I mean and mean what I say.

*On this day…*
I will not tackle all my problems at once but
live moment to moment at my very best.

*On this day…*
I will live my life being assertive, not aggressive; being humble,
not proud; being confident to be exactly who I am.

*On this day…*
I will take care of my physical health. I will exercise
my mind, my body, and my spirit.

*On this day…*
I will be kind to those around me. I will be agreeable, finding no
fault with others. Nor will I try to improve or regulate others.

*On this day…*
I will remind myself that God has a special place in His
heart for me and a special purpose for me to fulfill in this world.

CARL DREIZLER AND MARY E. EHEMANN
FROM "52 WAYS TO LOSE WEIGHT".

CONTENTMENT

# HOW ATTITUDE AFFECTS US

Our attitude at the beginning of a job will affect
the outcome of the job more than anything else.

Our attitude toward life determines life's attitude toward us.

Our attitude toward others will determine their attitude toward us.

Before we can achieve the kind of life we want,
we must think, act, walk, talk, and conduct ourselves in
ways characteristic of who we ultimately wish to become.

The higher we go in any organization of value,
the better the attitude we'll find.

Holding successful, positive thoughts in our minds
will make all the difference in the world.

If we always make a person feel needed, important, and
appreciated, he or she will return this attitude to us.

Part of a good attitude is to look for the best in new ideas.
So look for good ideas everywhere.
We will find them in the most wonderful places:
on the bumpers of cars, on restaurant menus, in books, in travel,
out of the innocent mouths of children.

Don't broadcast personal problems.
It probably won't help you, and it cannot help others.

Don't talk about your health unless it's good.

Radiate the attitude of well-being.
Don't be embarrassed to share visions, desires, and goals.

Treat everyone with whom you come in contact as a fellow member
of the human race—with all the rights, duties, and privileges thereof.
The Golden Rule still applies:
Do unto others as you would have them do unto you.

TED W. ENGSTROM
FROM "MOTIVATION TO LAST A LIFETIME"

# HOW TO FORFEIT PEACE

1.

*Resent God's ways.*

2.

*Worry as much as possible.*

3.

*Pray only about things you can't manage by yourself.*

4.

*Refuse to accept what God gives.*

5.

*Look for peace elsewhere than in Him.*

6.

*Try to rule your own life.*

7.

*Doubt God's Word.*

8.

*Carry all your cares.*

ELISABETH ELLIOT
FROM "KEEP A QUIET HEART"

# HOW TO FIND PEACE

### 1.
*"Great peace have they which love thy law: and nothing shall offend them."*
PSALM 119:165 KJV

### 2.
*"Don't worry over anything whatever."*
PHILIPPIANS 4:6, PHILLIPS

### 3.
*"In everything make your requests known to God in prayer and petition with thanksgiving. Then the peace of the God...will keep guard over your hearts."*
PHILIPPIANS 4:6, 7, NEB

### 4.
*"Take my yoke upon you and learn from me...and you will find rest."*
MATTHEW 11:29, NIV

### 5.
*"Peace is my parting gift to you, my own peace, such as the world cannot give."*
JOHN 14:27, NEB

### 6.
*"Let the peace of Christ rule in your hearts."*
COLOSSIANS 3:15, NIV

### 7.
*"Now the God of hope fill you will all joy and peace in believing."*
ROMANS 15:13, KJV

### 8.
*"Cast all your cares on him, for you are his charge."*
1 PETER 5:7, NEB

ELISABETH ELLIOT
FROM "KEEP A QUIET HEART"

# 12 REASONS TO PRAY

1.
It encourages others.

2.
It reminds you of spiritual values.

3.
It gives hope.

4.
It helps you feel better.

5.
It allows you to let go of situations.

6.
It provides comfort.

7.
It relaxes you and reduces anxiety.

8.
It builds faith.

9.
It deepens character.

10.
It broadens your perspective.

11.
It brings you closer to God.

12.
It works.

JOHN VAN DIEST, BOARD OF DIRECTORS
WALK THRU THE BIBLE MINISTRIES

# 12 THINGS TO PRAY FOR

**1.**

For a growing relationship with God

**2.**

For positive relationships
with your family members

**3.**

For energy and enthusiasm
for your work or career

**4.**

For wisdom to make
right and wise decisions

**5.**

For your service to your
church and community

**6.**

For the special needs of
your family and friends

**7.**

For the spiritual lives
of your church leaders

**8.**

For wisdom for our government leaders

**9.**

For the moral integrity
of today's young people

**10.**

For the safety of those
serving in our armed forces

**11.**

For a lasting peace
among peoples and nations

**12.**

For the opportunity to
be a blessing to someone today

J. CARL LANEY,
PROFESSOR OF BIBLICAL LITERATURE, WESTERN SEMINARY

# I'M THANKFUL FOR...

Air and autumn and animals.
Babies and breath and beauty.
Children and compassion and creativity.
Daylight and dew and daffodils.
Emotions and energy and enthusiasm.
Faith and family and friends.
Grandparents and grandchildren and God.
Hands and health and hope.
Ice cream and intelligence and intuition.
Joy and journeys and jokes.
Kindness and kisses and kittens.
Love and laughter and leaves.
Mothers and music and memories.
Night and nature and neighbors.
Order and oranges and oceans.
Peace and patience and prayer.
Quiet and quality and questions.
Rain and rest and romance.
Sunshine and smiles and stars.
Time and teachers and trees.
Unity and understanding and uniqueness.
Vision and values and vacations.
Winter and water and wisdom.
eXcitement and eXpression and eXperience.
Youth and yearning and yesterday.
Zest and zip and zeal.

TAMI STEPHENS
MOTHER OF THREE

# WHAT WE CAN CONTROL

WE CANNOT CONTROL

the length of our life, but we can
control its width and depth.

WE CANNOT CONTROL

the contour of our countenance,
but we can control its expression.

WE CANNOT CONTROL

the other person's annoying habits,
but we can do something about our own.

WE CANNOT CONTROL

the distance our head is above the ground,
but we can control the height of the contents we feed into it.

*God help us do something about what we can
control and leave all else in the hands of God!*

JOHN LAWRENCE
FROM "THE SEVEN LAWS OF THE HARVEST"

# YOU'RE BLESSED WHEN...

### YOU'RE BLESSED

when you're at the end of your rope. With less of you there is more of God and his rule.

### YOU'RE BLESSED

when you feel you've lost what is most dear to you. Only then can you be embraced by the One most dear to you.

### YOU'RE BLESSED

when you're content with just who you are—no more, no less. That's the moment you find yourselves proud owners of everything that can't be bought.

### YOU'RE BLESSED

when you've worked up a good appetite for God. He's food and drink in the best meal you'll ever eat.

### YOU'RE BLESSED

when you care. At the moment of being "care-full," you find your-selves cared for.

YOU'RE BLESSED

when you get your inside world—your mind and heart—put right. Then you can see God in the outside world.


YOU'RE BLESSED

when you can show people how to cooperate instead of compete or fight. That's when you discover who you really are, and your place in God's family.


YOU'RE BLESSED

when your commitment to God provokes persecution. The persecution drives you even deeper into God's kingdom.


NO ONLY THAT—

count yourselves blessed every time people put you down or throw you out or speak lies about you to discredit Me. What it means is that the truth is too close for comfort and they are uncomfortable.

JESUS, MATTHEW 5: 3-11
PARAPHRASED BY EUGENE PETERSON IN "THE MESSAGE"

# STANDING STRONG

## 9

### Getting through the struggles of life

# CHOOSE TO...

CHOOSE TO LOVE . . . . . . . .rather than hate.

CHOOSE TO SMILE . . . . . . . .rather than frown.

CHOOSE TO BUILD . . . . . . . .rather than destroy.

CHOOSE TO PERSEVERE . . . . . . . .rather than quit.

CHOOSE TO PRAISE . . . . . . . .rather than gossip.

CHOOSE TO HEAL . . . . . . . .rather than wound.

CHOOSE TO GIVE . . . . . . . .rather than grasp.

CHOOSE TO ACT . . . . . . . .rather than delay.

CHOOSE TO FORGIVE . . . . . . . .rather than curse.

CHOOSE TO PRAY . . . . . . . .rather than despair.

AUTHOR UNKNOWN

# WINNING OVER WORRY

1.

*Don't give up. Hope in God.*

2.

*Walk by faith, not by sight.*

3.

*Take time out for a good laugh.*

4.

*Use the Bible as a window to see your world.*

5.

*Never trouble trouble until trouble troubles you.*

6.

*Make choices based on God's Word.*

7.

*Give thanks to the Lord, for he is good.*

8.

*Ask for God's strength to get you through.*

9.

*Stop and enjoy the moment.*

10.

*Pray as if everything depended upon God—it does.*

LINDA SHEPHERD
FROM "LOVE'S LITTLE RECIPES FOR LIFE"

# IN THE EYE OF THE STORM

*Love God more than you fear hell.*

*Once a week, let a child take you on a walk.*

*Make major decisions in a cemetery.*

*When no one is watching, live as if someone is.*

*Succeed at home first.*

*Don't spend tomorrow's money today.*

*Pray twice as much as you fret.*

*Listen twice as much as you speak.*

*Only harbor a grudge when God does.*

*Never outgrow your love of sunsets.*

*Treat people like angels; you will meet some and help make some.*

*'Tis wiser to err on the side of generosity than on the side of scrutiny.*

*God has forgiven you; you'd be wise to do the same.*

*When you can't trace God's hand, trust his heart.*

*Toot your own horn and the notes will be flat.*

*Don't feel guilty for God's goodness.*

*The book of life is lived in chapters, so know your page number.*

*Never let the important be the victim of the trivial.*

*Live your liturgy.*

MAX LUCADO
FROM "IN THE EYE OF THE STORM"

# OVERCOMING DEPRESSION
# & DISCOURAGEMENT

### 1.

*Visit your physician.* Depression might be a symptom of a physical problem. Hypothyroidism, hypoglycemia, an amino imbalance, an endocrine imbalance, or a viral infection can all cause depression.

### 2.

*Eat healthy.* Eat plenty of fruits and vegetables. Avoid caffeine, sugar, junk food, and especially alcohol.

### 3.

*Get enough sleep.* Exhaustion adds to depression. Sleep refreshes the body and uplifts the spirit. But too much sleep can be a sign of avoiding important issues that can get you depressed.

### 4.

*Be active.* Physical activity can lift you out of depression. Be active and enjoy the outdoors, especially when it's sunny. Avoid too much television or too many passive activities. Activity energizes.

### 5.

*Be social.* Surrounding yourself with people, especially positive people, can keep your mind off your problems and distract you from feeling sorry for yourself. Social interactions help pull you from your depression.

### 6.

*Do fun activities.* When you are depressed you don't want to do anything; nothing sounds enjoyable. But getting out and doing what you used to enjoy will improve your attitude and after a while you will have fun.

### 7.

*Write out your feelings.* Emotions trapped inside you increase depression. Getting them out on paper can release the internal pressure. Write about your anger, grief, confusion, loss, stress, or anything else that's bothering you.

### 8.

*Surround yourself with positives.* Fill your life with positive people, positive music, positive books, and positive situations. Stay away from negatives. Positives make you feel better, and as you feel better the depression loses its grip.

### 9.

*Check out your negative self-talk.* Listen to what you're saying to yourself. If you are saying negative things about yourself, your world, or the future, it will make you feel worse. Putting a positive spin on life will make you feel better.

### 10.

*Make plans and dreams for the future.* Dreaming about the future can be exciting. Make a list of all the things you wish to do in the future and then plan how to make them a reality.

### 11.

*Develop your faith.* Faith in God provides hope. It lifts a person above the frustrations and traumas of life. It also gives meaning to our existence. Faith pulls a person above depression and provides perspective to difficulties.

### 12.

*Get help if the depression persists.* Meet with a pastor if there are spiritual issues or a counselor if there are emotional problems or your physician for medication. It is a sign of wisdom and courage to seek help if needed.

DR. STEVE STEPHENS
PSYCHOLOGIST AND SEMINAR SPEAKER

STANDING STRONG

# A POSITIVE FOCUS

LET YOUR MIND DWELL ON THESE EIGHT THINGS...

*Whatever is true*

*Whatever is noble*

*Whatever is right*

*Whatever is pure*

*Whatever is lovely*

*Whatever is admirable*

*Whatever is excellent*

*Whatever is praiseworthy*

PHILIPPIANS 4:8 (NIV)

# BE GOOD TO YOU

BE YOURSELF . . . . . . . . truthfully.

ACCEPT YOURSELF . . . . . . . . gratefully.

VALUE YOURSELF . . . . . . . . joyfully.

FORGIVE YOURSELF . . . . . . . . completely.

TREAT YOURSELF . . . . . . . . generously.

BALANCE YOURSELF . . . . . . . . harmoniously.

BLESS YOURSELF . . . . . . . . abundantly.

TRUST YOURSELF . . . . . . . . confidently.

LOVE YOURSELF . . . . . . . . wholeheartedly.

EMPOWER YOURSELF . . . . . . . . prayerfully.

GIVE YOURSELF . . . . . . . . enthusiastically.

EXPRESS YOURSELF . . . . . . . . radiantly.

AUTHOR UNKNOWN

# STRESS BUSTERS

### 1.
#### DEVELOP ORDER

*Tidy up. Put things away. Toss clutter. You can restore a
sense of calm to a room with a thirty-minute "sort and dump."*

### 2.
#### DIVERT YOUR FOCUS

*Diversions give the mind a break from problem solving
and burden bearing. It is impossible to be consumed with
worry when something else is captivating your interest.*

### 3.
#### DIFFUSE

*Push the pressures out of your body through
twenty minutes of aerobic exercise.*

### 4.
#### DEBRIEF

*Talk out your tension with a safe and trusted friend.*

### 5.
#### DIVERSIFY

*Change channels in your brain.
Problem solving is more effective when the mind frequently rests
from a problem rather than obsessing on it continuously.*

### 6.
#### DELIBERATELY REST

*Schedule several five-minute slots during the day to "let down,"
and slow the mind and body. Listen to relaxing music.
Pray and meditate on Scriptures that soothe the soul.*

### 7.
#### DEAL WITH UNFINISHED BUSINESS

*Make amends whenever possible.
Grant forgiveness rather than nursing grudges.*

## 8.
### DECIDE TO TRUST

*One of the best prescriptions for fear is to say,*
*"God, I choose to trust you."*

## 9.
### DEDICATE YOURSELF TO THE BASICS

*To see clearly in the midst of blinding stress:*
*Sleep eight to nine hours a night;*
*Eat well-balanced meals;*
*Exercise twenty to thirty minutes, three times a week.*

## 10.
### DISENGAGE

*When overwhelmed, step back, buy yourself some time,*
*and stop trying so hard. Everything doesn't have to be "fixed" today.*

## 11.
### DIG IN

*Avoidance heightens anxiety. Evaluate what can be done and do it.*
*Don't get stuck in the quicksand of an "all or nothing" approach.*

## 12.
### DON'T BE A "TYPE E" PERSON

*No one was designed to be Everything to Everybody.*
*Only God can fill that job description.*

PAM VREDEVELT
LICENSED PROFESSIONAL COUNSELOR

# ARE YOU DOING TOO MUCH?

IF YOU'RE THINKING THAT YOUR LIFESTYLE
NEEDS SIMPLIFYING, TRY ASKING YOURSELF THESE QUESTIONS:

*Have you ever missed an important event in your child's life
because of a conflicting obligation for which you volunteered?*

*Do you feel that reading or relaxing is a waste of time?*

*Does your family have trouble finding time to spend together?*

*Are the storage spaces in your home overflowing because you don't
have time to clean out what's been outgrown, broken, or used up?*

*Do you spend most of your day feeling tired?*

*Are you afraid to say "no" to an opportunity,
fearing it will never come again?*

*Do you give your children material items to make up
for denying them your time and energy?*

*Do you often find you've overscheduled yourself,
underestimating the time needed for each event?*

RAMONA RICHARDS
FROM "HOMELIFE" MAGAZINE

# EIGHT QUESTIONS TO ASK BEFORE SAYING YES

### 1.
*Do I really understand this commitment?*

### 2.
*How does this fit into my current goals and priorities?*

### 3.
*Do I have the time, energy, and resources?*

### 4.
*What impact will this have on me in a year? in five years? in ten years?*

### 5.
*How will this impact those I love? Who will it help? Who will it hurt?*

### 6.
*What do my friends and family think?*

### 7.
*Can someone else do it better?*

### 8.
*Do I really want to say yes?*

ALICE GRAY AND DR. STEVE STEPHENS
SEMINAR SPEAKERS

# NINE GOALS FOR AUTHENTIC GROWTH

1.

*Have a passion for excellence.*

2.

*Ask, listen, and hear—to determine the wants, needs,
and possibilities of all with whom I come in contact.*

3.

*Provide an example of commitment and integrity.*

4.

*Follow a path of continual empowerment for myself and others.*

5.

*Constantly focus on strengths of all with whom I come in contact.*

6.

*Cultivate optimum physical, mental, and spiritual fitness.*

7.

*Lead as I would like to be led.*

8.

*Savor the flavor of each passing moment.*

9.

*Infuse every thought and relationship
with faith, hope, love, and gratitude.*

JOE D. BATTEN
FROM "NEW MAN" MAGAZINE

# TEN BELIEFS THAT LEAD TO ANGER

### 1.
*If I want something, I should have it—no matter
whom it hurts or how I get it.*

### 2.
*It is terrible and unjust to be kept waiting. I can't accept excuses.*

### 3.
*I must never be uncomfortable or frustrated. I can avoid distress at all cost.*

### 4.
*I have a right to be angry when others hurt my feelings,
cause me discomfort, or disappoint me.*

### 5.
*If I don't sleep well or if I've had a bad day,
I have a right to be irritable and others should leave me alone.*

### 6.
*My parents always helped me.
Others shouldn't expect me to do it by myself.*

### 7.
*I detest it when others think their way is the only way—
even if they are the bosses.*

### 8.
*I must succeed at everything I choose to do. There is no room for failure.*

### 9.
*I deserve immediate gratification. I am entitled to "It."*

### 10.
*Other motorists need to get out of my way.*

GLENDA HOTTON
MARRIAGE AND FAMILY THERAPIST

# DEALING WITH ANGER

### 1.
#### ADMIT YOUR ANGER.

*If you're angry, be honest with yourself about it.*

### 2.
#### EVALUATE YOUR ANGER.

*Ask yourself, "What triggers my anger?*
*When am I most likely to feel anger?"*

### 3.
#### CHOOSE YOUR PERCEPTION.

*Slow down and put the problem in perspective.*
*Frame the situation in as positive a way as you can.*

### 4.
#### CALM YOURSELF DOWN.

*If your anger is getting out of control, lower your voice,*
*sit down, and breathe deeply. If you still can't calm*
*down, remove yourself from the situation.*

### 5.
#### WATCH YOUR WORDS AND ACTIONS.

*When you're angry, it is easy to say and do things you will*
*later regret. Watch carefully what you say; once those words are*
*out of your mouth, you can never take them back.*

## 6.

### WORK YOUR ANGER OUT.

*Anger produces adrenaline and adrenaline seeks release. You need to work your anger out. Go for a drive, weed a garden, chop wood, write a letter, or take a walk.*

## 7.

### TALK ABOUT YOUR ANGER.

*Take responsibility for your feelings. Be direct and honest without blaming or attacking. If you're overreacting, admit it. The better you can communicate about your anger, the more you can control it.*

## 8.

### DON'T LET THE SUN GO DOWN ON YOUR ANGER.

*Commit yourself to resolving your anger as soon as possible. Unresolved anger turns into bitterness, revenge, or both. The sooner you handle your anger, the better.*

## 9.

### SEEK HELP.

*If your anger persists or is out of control, get help immediately. Talk to a counselor or a pastor or a physician and develop a more intensive plan.*

DR. STEVE STEPHENS
FROM "MARRIAGE: EXPERIENCE THE BEST"

# THE WORLD NEEDS PEOPLE...

Who cannot be bought;

Whose word is their bond;

Who put character above wealth;

Who possess opinions and a will;

Who are larger than their vocations;

Who do not hesitate to take chances;

Who will not lose their individuality in a crowd;

Who will be as honest in small things as in great things;

Who will make no compromise with wrong;

Whose ambitions are not confined to their own selfish desires;

Who will not say they do it "because everybody else does it;"

Who are true to their friends through good report and evil report,
in adversity as well as prosperity;

Who do not believe that shrewdness, cunning, and
hardheadedness are the best qualities for winning success;

Who are not ashamed or afraid to stand for the truth when it is unpopular;

Who can say "no" with emphasis, although all the rest of the world says "yes."

TED W. ENGSTROM
FROM "MOTIVATION TO LAST A LIFETIME"

# FAMILY FUN

*Relax and enjoy*

# TOP 10 FREE TOYS FOR CHILDREN

**1.**
*Cape made from bath towel*

**2.**
*Empty squeeze bottles for tub toys*

**3.**
*Arm sling made from dish towel*

**4.**
*Pretend grocery store stocked with empty food packages*
*(canned goods, cereal boxes, spices, etc.)*

**5.**
*Binoculars made from empty toilet paper tubes taped together*
*(add plastic food wrap lenses for professional effect)*

**6.**
*Puppets made from the stray socks piling up in the laundry room*

**7.**
*Sewing cards made from styrofoam meat trays and old shoelaces*

**8.**
*Pretend post office stocked with junk mail*

**9.**
*Tent made from sheets and blankets*

**10.**
*Empty cardboard box*

*Honorary mention: Own library card*

CRYSTAL KIRGISS, MOTHER OF THREE BOYS
COLUMNIST FOR THE "DETROIT LAKES TRIBUNE"

# FAMILY GUIDELINES FOR TELEVISION

### 1.
*Decide ahead of time what you want to watch.*

### 2.
*Include your children when setting up guidelines.*

### 3.
*Turn the TV off during meals.*

### 4.
*Set up a limit of how much to watch each day with a goal
to decrease rather than increase your viewing time.*

### 5.
*Watch together as a couple or a family (not alone).*

### 6.
*Always do homework or chores first (a suggested rule for every member
of the family—one hour of reading before one hour of TV).*

### 7.
*Set rules for babysitters.*

### 8.
*Acquire a good collection of family videos as alternative choices.*

### 9.
*Pay attention to rating guides.*

### 10.
*Talk about what you watch.*

### 11.
*Evaluate what you saw in terms of violence, language,
sexual content, morality, respect for individuals, and accuracy.*

### 12.
*Take advantage of viewing time together to snuggle and rub backs.*

ALICE GRAY, DR. STEVE STEPHENS, AND JOHN VAN DIEST
SEMINAR SPEAKERS

# FAMILY GUIDELINES FOR USING THE INTERNET

YOUR KIDS MAY NOT BE SAFE DRIVING THROUGH THE VIRTUAL VILLAGE ALONE. HERE ARE SOME TIPS TO KEEP THEM FROM SEEING THE SEEDIER SIDE OF CYBERSPACE.

*Keep your computer in a commonly visible area of the home.*

*Encourage your family to telecommute together.*

*Avoid late-night Internet surfing.*

*Limit the number of minutes each family member can spend on-line.*
*Periodically review file names of the documents your children download*

*Don't roam aimlessly. Always have a definite destination in mind.*

*Decide family standards for what on-line entertainment and*
*communication is acceptable. Explain the rules clearly*
*and stick to them. Be sure to include these three nevers:*

### 1.
*Never* give out personal information over the
computer. This includes full names, addresses, phone
numbers, or any financial data (credit card numbers, etc.).

### 2.
*Never* respond to anyone who leaves
obnoxious, lewd, or threatening e-mail.

### 3.
*Never* set up a face-to-face meeting with anyone
you meet via bulletin boards or chat forums.

"NEW MAN" MAGAZINE

# THE EIGHT BEST SURPRISES
# A KID EVER HAD

### 1.

*Pajama Ride*—One night, after the kids are in their pajamas and tucked into bed, wait about ten minutes, race into their rooms, flip on the light, and yell, "Pajama ride!" Wrap a blanket around them, toss them in the car, and go to a Dairy Queen for a hot fudge sundae. Your kids will love the memory, they'll get to see Mom and Dad act crazy, and you'll have a wonderful opportunity to talk with them about what's going on in their lives.

### 2.

*Water Fight*—When was the last time you asked your kids to help you wash the car, and then got everyone into a big water fight? Is it dumb? You bet—and an absolute riot. (We've got friends who are still talking about a family water fight we had six years ago!) The chance for them to see their parents have fun makes it memorable.

### 3.

*Scavenger Hunt*—Wake your kids up one morning and announce they've got an important task. After breakfast, they'll have two hours to find everything on your list (a red button, a yellow rose, a Beanie Baby, two jokers, a picture of a mountain, a penny from the 70s, a mattress advertisement, etc.—the sillier the better!). The fun is in the hunt—and in the chance to let everyone tell their stories at the end of the game.

### 4.

*Build a Fort*—Take the time to build something with your kids, be it a tree house, clubhouse, backyard tent, or even a living room fort made of couch cushions. There is something about the memory of working together and building a structure that stays with children.

## 5.

*Kids-in-Charge Night*—Put your children in charge some Saturday. Let them choose what you'll do in the afternoon, then ask them to set the table and give them simple recipes to cook for dinner. Use an easy menu (like spaghetti or pancakes) and let them go at it. The lesson will be worth the mess! After dinner, guide them through washing dishes, sorting laundry, emptying the trash, and sewing on buttons. During these activities, talk with your kids about the importance of fulfilling responsibilities.

## 6.

*Notes in Lunch Box*—Write an encouraging note to each of your children and stick them in their lunch boxes. If you're really brave, add a cartoon. An unexpected positive word can sometimes make a memory that lasts a lifetime.

## 7.

*Surprise Party*—Throw a surprise party. Make a cake, hang decorations, and invite your child's friends (make sure they keep it a secret). If it's for a birthday, that's great...but it doesn't have to be for anything special. Just the thought that you would go to the trouble of creating a surprise will be enough to make it memorable.

## 8.

*Day Off from School*—One day, after one of your children has received a good report card, show up at school and say, "Sorry, but I've got to take you out of school today. I need you to do something important with me." Then take him or her fishing. That's right: fishing. Sometimes a day with Mom or Dad is more important than a day with the teacher. (If you can't take the entire day, make it a lunch date!)

JERRY "CHIP" AND PATTI MACGREGOR
CONDENSED FROM "FAMILY TIMES: GROWING TOGETHER IN FUN AND FAITH"

# 20 FUN ACTIVITIES

## 1.
Bake cookies.

## 2.
Help a neighbor.

## 3.
Enjoy nature (i.e. watch for animals, set up a bird feeder, get an ant farm, collect bugs, find shapes in the clouds, or study the stars).

## 4.
Visit a zoo or museum or carnival.

## 5.
Create a painting or a poster.

## 6.
Put on a play or puppet show.

## 7.
Find something to collect (shells, coins, rocks, sports cards, anything).

## 8.
Plant a garden.

## 9.
Collect cans and bottles and give the money to charity.

## 10.
Fly a kite.

## 11.
Take flowers and a card to someone sick or lonely.

**12.**

*Read books aloud.*

**13.**

*Make giant pictures on your driveway with sidewalk chalk.*

**14.**

*Do a talent show.*

**15.**

*Go on a hike or bicycle ride.*

**16.**

*Look at family photographs or videos.*

**17.**

*Tell stories.*

**18.**

*Make family cards (for Christmas, Valentine's Day,
Thanksgiving, and birthdays).*

**19.**

*Paint each other's faces.*

**20.**

*Sing songs and/or make up songs.*

TAMI STEPHENS
MOTHER OF THREE

# 48 GREAT BOOKS TO READ ALOUD

1. *Christie* . . . . . . . . . . . . . . . . . . . . . . . .by Catherine Marshall
2. *Paddle to the Sea* . . . . . . . . . . . . . .by Holling Clancy Holling
3. *Where the Red Fern Grows* . . . . . . . . . . . . . .by Wilson Rawls
4. *Caddie Woodlawn* . . . . . . . . . . . . . . . . .by Carol Ryrie Brink
5. *Homer Price* . . . . . . . . . . . . . . . . . . . .by Robert McClosky
6. *The Cooper Kids Adventure series* . . . . . . . . . . .by Frank Peretti
7. *The Secret Garden* . . . . . . . . . . .by Frances Hodgson Burnett
8. *The Baker Street Mysteries* . . . . . . . .by Jake and Luke Thoene
9. *Ramona series* . . . . . . . . . . . . . . . . . . . .by Beverly Cleary
10. *Mary Poppins* . . . . . . . . . . . . . . . . . . . . . .by P. L. Travers
11. *A Wrinkle in Time* . . . . . . . . . . . . . . .by Madeleine L'Engle
12. *The Mixed-up Files of Mrs. Basil F. Frankweiler*
    . . . . . . . . . . . . . . . . . . . . . . . . . . . . . .by E.L. Konigsburg
13. *The Chronicles of Narnia* . . . . . . . . . . . . . . . .by C.S. Lewis
14. *Little Women* . . . . . . . . . . . . . . . . . . .by Louisa May Alcott
15. *The Girl of the Limberlost* . . . . . . . . . . .by Gene Stratton Porter
16. *House at Pooh Corner* . . . . . . . . . . . . . . . . . .by A. A. Milne
17. *Little House on the Prairie* . . . . . . . . . . .by Laura Ingalls Wilder
18. *Charlotte's Web* . . . . . . . . . . . . . . . . . . . .by E. B. White
19. *Anne of Green Gables* . . . . . . . . . . . . . .by L. M. Montgomery
20. *Gentle Ben* . . . . . . . . . . . . . . . . . . . . . . .by Walt Morey
21. *The Boxcar Children* . . . . . . . . . . .by Gertrude Chandler Warner
22. *Stone Fox* . . . . . . . . . . . . . . . . .by John Reynolds Gardiner
23. *Birdie's Lighthouse* . . . . . . . . . . . . . . . .by Deborah Hopkinson
24. *Heidi* . . . . . . . . . . . . . . . . . . . . . . . . .by Johanna Spyri

JANICE BYRAM
SCHOOL TEACHER

# HOW TO CHOOSE A
# VIDEO FOR YOUR FAMILY

## 1.
### CHECK THE RATING.

*Unrated means unknown. You have no idea what you are getting.*

If the video is rated, you'll find it on the back side of the jacket box. "G" means the movie is suitable for all audiences. "PG" means parental guidance is suggested. "PG13" often contains significant doses of sex, foul language, and violence. "R" means restricted, with no one under seventeen allowed without a parent or adult guardian.

## 2.
### ASK THE RIGHT QUESTIONS.

*Even when a rating is displayed on the box, discernment is crucial in choosing a videocassette. The following questions will help you.*

What is the premise of the movie? What message does the film communicate? You can often find the premise on the jacket of the videotape. Remember—you have to read between the lines.

Who is the hero and what kind of role model is he or she?
How is religion portrayed?
How is the world portrayed?
How is love portrayed?
How is the family portrayed?

## 3.
### KNOW WHAT YOU WANT TO RENT BEFORE
### YOU WALK INTO THE STORE.

*If you do find yourself browsing,
head for the "classics" or "musicals" sections.
They stand a better chance of being good for family viewing.*

## 4.
### TOTALLY AVOID HORROR MOVIES AND
### TEEN "SEXPLOITATION" FILMS

TED BAEHR
CONDENSED FROM "THE WAR CRY" MAGAZINE

# 20 GREAT CHILDREN'S MOVIES
## (MOST FOR AGE SIX AND OLDER)

1. Adventures of Milo and Otis

2. Anne of Green Gables

3. Babe

4. Beauty and the Beast

5. Benji

6. The Black Stallion

7. Charlie Brown's All Stars

8. Heidi

9. Homeward Bound

10. Lady and the Tramp

11. Mary Poppins

12. Miracle on 34th Street

13. National Velvet

14. Oliver and Company

15. Pinocchio

16. Pollyanna

17. Prince of Egypt

18. Toy Story

19. A Tree Grows in Brooklyn

20. The Velveteen Rabbit

JOHN EVANS, EDITOR "FAMILY VIDEO GUIDE"
(THE ABOVE LIST WAS SELECTED BY THE EDITORS FROM OVER 1000
RECOMMENDED VIDEO MOVIES BASED ON TRADITIONAL FAMILY VALUES.)

# 20 GREAT FAMILY MOVIES

## (FOR AGE 12 AND OLDER)

1. Ben Hur

2. Chariots of Fire

3. Christy

4. Driving Miss Daisy

5. Gone with the Wind

6. The Good Earth

7. Great Expectations (1946)

8. Inn of Sixth Happiness

9. It's a Wonderful Life

10. Little Women (1994)

11. Mr. Smith Goes to Washington

12. North by Northwest

13. The Quiet Man

14. The Preacher's Wife (1996)

15. The Sound of Music

16. Sounder

17. The Yearling

18. To Kill a Mockingbird

19. Twenty Thousand

    Leagues Under the Sea

20. Where the Red Fern Grows

JOHN EVANS, EDITOR "FAMILY VIDEO GUIDE"
(THE ABOVE LIST WAS SELECTED BY THE EDITORS FROM OVER 1000
RECOMMENDED VIDEO MOVIES BASED ON TRADITIONAL FAMILY VALUES.)

# 20 GREAT TABLE GAMES

1. Candyland

2. Chutes and Ladders

3. Sorry

4. Pictionary

5. Concentration

6. Checkers

7. Chess

8. Dominoes

9. Chinese Checkers

10. Scrabble

11. Scattergories

12. Boggle

13. Payday

14. Life

15. Yatzee

16. Cribbage

17. Jenga

18. Uno

19. Old Maid

20. Monopoly

TAMI STEPHENS
MOTHER OF THREE

# FAMILY LIFE

*Growing together*

11

# THE JOB OF PARENTS

*Parents can and must:*

TRAIN,

SHAPE,

MOLD,

CORRECT,

GUIDE,

PUNISH,

REWARD,

INSTRUCT,

WARN,

TEACH,

AND LOVE

*their kids during the formative years.*

DR. JAMES C. DOBSON
FROM "PARENTING ISN'T FOR COWARDS"

# 10 FAMILY COMMITMENTS

1.
*I will not hit.*

2.
*I will not keep secrets.*

3.
*I will not lie.*

4.
*I will not use bad language.*

5.
*I will not use drugs, and if I know somebody
who is using drugs, I'll try to help them.*

6.
*I will treat others with respect.*

7.
*If I make a mess, I'll clean it up.*

8.
*I'll pick up my clothes and keep my room neat.*

9.
*I'll talk to Mom and Dad about my problems.*

10.
*I'll do my homework before I go out to play.*

GREG CYNAUMON, PH.D.
FROM "HOW TO AVOID ALIENATING YOUR KIDS IN 10 EASY STEPS"

# SIX STEPS TO SUCCESSFUL COMMUNICATION

Thinking of the word "ladder" will help you remember these steps.

L ook at the person speaking to you.

A sk questions.

D on't interrupt.

D on't change the subject.

E mpathize.

R espond verbally and nonverbally.

AUTHOR UNKNOWN
AS CITED IN "MORE OF...THE BEST OF BITS & PIECES," ROB GILBERT, PH.D., ED.

# 20 CONVERSATION STARTERS

*Here are twenty questions you can use to
strike up a conversation with your kids:*

What was the neatest birthday present you ever received?

What makes you laugh?

What is your favorite food?

Where would you like to go for a vacation if you could go anyplace
in the whole world?

If you had to move and could take only three things with you, what
would you take?

How would you describe the "ideal" father or mother?

What is something you can do pretty well?

What is your favorite song?

What is your best friend like?

How would you describe yourself to someone who does not know you?

Has there been a time when you felt proud of yourself?

What kind of store would you like to own and operate?

If you received $5,000 as a gift—how would you spend it?

What is your favorite room in our house? Why?

What kind of a job do you want to have in twenty years?

What talent do you wish you had?

If someone could give you anything in the world for
your birthday—what would you like it to be?

What would you like to invent to make life better?

What is something that bugs you?

What kind of trophy would you like to win?

JERRY "CHIP" AND PATTI MACGREGOR
FROM "FAMILY TIMES: GROWING TOGETHER IN FUN AND FAITH"

# WHY DIVORCE HURTS CHILDREN

## 1.

It signals the collapse of the family structure—the child feels alone and frightened. This loneliness can be acute and long remembered.

## 2.

A couple's capacity to be parents is diminished. They are preoccupied with their own emotional survival during the critical months (or years) of the divorce.

## 3.

Divorce creates conflicts of loyalty in the children. Whose side do they take? They feel pulled by love and loyalty in both directions.

## 4.

Uncertainty about the future often causes deep-seated insecurity in children. Being dependent mainly on one parent can create a great deal of anxiety.

## 5.

Anger and resentment between parents, which is prevalent in most divorces, creates intense fear in the child. The younger he or she is, the more damaging the climate of anger can be.

## 6.

Children take upon themselves anxiety concerning their parents. They worry intensely about their mother in particular, with the departure of the father being a terrifying event.

## 7.

If the family moves, a child may lose an "at-home" parent, a home, a school, a church, and friends. Divorce represents the loss of so many things that a deep depression is almost inevitable. Yet most parents fail to recognize this depression in their children.

A prominent child psychologist, Dr. Lee Salk, has said, "The trauma of divorce is second only to death. Children sense a deep loss and feel they are suddenly vulnerable to forces beyond their control."

ARCHIBALD HART
CONDENSED FROM "MOODY" MAGAZINE

# 10 WAYS TO BE A GREAT DAD

### 1.
#### RESPECT YOUR CHILDREN'S MOTHER.

One of the best things a father can do for his children is to respect their mother. If you are married, keep your marriage strong and vital. If you're not married, it is still important to respect and support the mother of your children.

### 2.
#### SPEND TIME WITH YOUR CHILDREN.

How a father spends his time tells his children what's important to him. If you always seem too busy for your children, they will feel neglected no matter what you say.

### 3.
#### EARN THE RIGHT TO BE HEARD.

All too often the only time a father speaks to his children is when they have done something wrong. Begin talking with your kids when they are very young so that difficult subjects will be easier to handle as they get older. Take time and listen to their ideas and problems.

### 4.
#### DISCIPLINE WITH LOVE.

All children need guidance and discipline, not as punishment, but to set reasonable limits. Remind your children of the consequences of their actions and provide meaningful rewards for desirable behavior.

### 5.
#### BE A ROLE MODEL.

Fathers are role models to their kids, whether they realize it or not. A girl who spends time with a loving father grows up knowing she deserves to be treated with respect by boys, and what to look for in a husband. Fathers can teach sons what is important in life by demonstrating honesty, humility, and responsibility.

## 6.
### BE A TEACHER.

Too many fathers think teaching is something others do. But a father who teaches his children about right and wrong, and encourages them to do their best, will see his children make good choices.

## 7.
### EAT TOGETHER AS A FAMILY.

Sharing a meal together (breakfast, lunch, or dinner) can be an important part of healthy family life. In addition to providing some structure in a busy day, it gives kids the chance to talk about what they are doing and want to do.

## 8.
### READ TO YOUR CHILDREN.

Begin reading to your children when they are very young. When they are older, encourage them to read on their own. Instilling your children with a love for reading is one of the best ways to ensure they will have a lifetime of personal and career growth.

## 9.
### SHOW AFFECTION.

Children need security that comes from knowing they are wanted, accepted, and loved by their family. Parents, especially fathers, need to feel both comfortable and willing to hug their children. Showing affection every day is the best way to let your children know that you love them.

## 10.
### REALIZE THAT A FATHER'S JOB IS NEVER DONE.

Even after children are grown and ready to leave home, they will still look to their fathers for wisdom and advice. Whether it's continued schooling, a new job, or a wedding, fathers continue to play an essential part in the lives of their children as they grow and, perhaps, marry and build their own families.

THE NATIONAL FATHERHOOD INITIATIVE

# HELP FOR DISCOURAGED PARENTS

### 1.
You are not to blame for the temperament with which your child was born. He is simply a tough kid to handle and your task is to rise to the challenge.

### 2.
He is in greater danger because of his inclination to test the limits and scale the walls. Your utmost diligence and wisdom will be required to deal with him.

### 3.
If you fail to understand his lust for power and independence, you can exhaust your resources and bog down in guilt. It will benefit no one.

### 4.
If it is not already too late, by all means, take charge of your babies. Hold tightly to the reins of authority in the early days, and build an attitude of respect during your brief window of opportunity. You will need every ounce of "awe" you can get during the years to come. Once you have established your right to lead, begin to let go systematically, year by year.

### 5.

Don't panic, even during the storms of adolescence. Better times are ahead. A radical turnaround usually occurs in the early twenties.

### 6.

Stay on your child's team, even when it appears to be a *losing* team. You'll have the rest of your life to enjoy mutual fellowship if you don't overreact to frustration now.

### 7.

Give him time to find himself, even if he appears not to be searching.

### 8.

Most importantly, I urge you to hold your children before the Lord in fervent prayer throughout their years at home. I am convinced that there is no other source of confidence and wisdom in parenting.

DR. JAMES C. DOBSON
FROM "PARENTING ISN'T FOR COWARDS"

# FAMILY TEAM BUILDING

## 1.
### GREAT GOALS

*Promote activities in which siblings
must work together to reach a goal.*

## 2.
### GAMES

*During family time, join the children as a team.*

## 3.
### WORKING TOGETHER

*Assign chores that must be completed with cooperation.*

## 4.
### CHARITY WORK

*Unite your children to reach out to the less fortunate.*

## 5.
### FUN PROJECTS

*Promote sibling activities such as large puzzles, birdhouses, or
craft kits to develop a sense of teamwork. Use limited supplies
such as glue and markers, so children will have to share.*

## 6.
### AN OFFERING FOR EVERY OCCASION

*Unite forces to create gifts, such as cookies,
for neighbors or presents for grandparents.*

## 7.
### BOOK TIME

*Have children read to each other, or have an older child read to a younger sibling. Also, make up your own "sibling" stories for your children. Have Super Brother save little sister from the scary bear, or add your children as characters to Bible stories.*

## 8.
### KING OR QUEEN FOR THE DAY

*Have one day a week be "Royal Kid Day."
One child is the king or queen and will receive special treatment. The other "servant" children will also enjoy themselves as they prepare food and games for the queen or king of the day.*

## 9.
### SPECIAL PARENT DAY

*Siblings will have tons of fun working together to fulfill the needs of the chosen adult. (This is great for the adults, too!)*

## 10.
### FAMILY TALENT NIGHT

*Encourage each child to shine like a star in front of the family. Tumbling acts, singing specials, or the presentation of school projects will bring claps and support from other siblings.*

TRICIA GOYER AND CINDY MCCORMICK MARTINUSEN
CONDENSED FROM "HOMELIFE" MAGAZINE

# BE A PARENT TEACHERS LIKE TO SEE

## 1.
### ESTABLISH A POSITIVE RELATIONSHIP

Try to work together. If you become acquainted with your child's teacher before problems occur, you will have a greater impact when a need arises.

## 2.
### GIVE HELP, NOT ADVICE

Most teachers need help, not more information. When helping, try to do what the teacher wants, not necessarily what you want.

## 3.
### SHOW APPRECIATION

Even in the most positive schools, an amazingly small number of parents (and students!) ever show appreciation. We all work harder for those who say thanks.

## 4.
### BE POSITIVE

If your child struggles, make the teacher aware of the problem and ask for suggestions. Don't be afraid to tell the teacher your plans and how she can help. Focus on changing your child, not the teacher, the school, or the child in the next seat.

### 5.
#### PICK YOUR BATTLES

Don't overlook important issues, but choose your battles carefully. Realize that if you fight, people get hurt. Is it worth it? Many battles aren't.

### 6.
#### RESPECT THE TEACHER

For a good idea of how you might be perceived by a teacher, ask yourself this question: What would the teacher's life be like if every parent did what I do?

### 7.
#### PRAY FOR THE TEACHER

If you multiply your needs as a parent times the teacher's twenty-five students, you will feel the need to pray for her.

JOE NEFF, DIRECTOR OF GUIDANCE AT WHEATON ACADEMY
CONDENSED FROM "FOCUS ON THE FAMILY" MAGAZINE

# FIVE MUSTS FOR EVERY FAMILY

### 1.
### AN ATTITUDE OF SERVICE.

*When family members help each other the whole family benefits.*

### 2.
### INTIMACY BETWEEN A HUSBAND AND WIFE.

*When a couple connects, it satisfies their inner longings and
gives the children a loving model of what family is all about.*

### 3.
### PARENTS WHO TEACH AND TRAIN.

*Guiding your children is a team effort.*

### 4.
### HUSBANDS WHO ARE LOVING LEADERS.

*A man needs to lead his wife and children in a
loving way and live his spiritual and moral values.
It inspires his family to do the same.*

### 5.
### CHILDREN WHO OBEY AND HONOR THEIR PARENTS.

*Kids need to learn that living by rules is good
for them and everyone around them.*

GARY CHAPMAN
FROM "FIVE SIGNS OF A FUNCTIONAL FAMILY"

# FAMILY VALUES

*Learning together*

**12**

# QUALITIES TO PASS ON
# TO YOUR CHILDREN

DETERMINATION . . . . . . . . . . . . . . . . . . . . . . . . ."Stick with it, regardless."

HONESTY . . . . . . . . . . . . . . . . . . . . . ."Speak and live the truth—always."

RESPONSIBILITY . . . . . . . . . . . . . . . . . . ."Be dependable, be trustworthy."

THOUGHTFULNESS . . . . . . . . . . . . . . . ."Think of others before yourself."

CONFIDENTIALITY . . . . . . . . . . . . . . . ."Don't tell secrets. Seal your lips."

PUNCTUALITY . . . . . . . . . . . . . . . . . . . . . . . . . . . . . . . . . . ."Be on time."

SELF-CONTROL . . . . . . . . . . . . . . . . . . . . ."When under stress, stay calm."

PATIENCE . . . . . . . . . . . . . . . . . . . . . . ."Fight irritability. Be willing to wait."

PURITY . . . . . . . . . . . . . . . ."Reject anything that lowers your standards."

COMPASSION . . . . . . . . . . . . . . . ."When another hurts, feel it with him."

DILIGENCE . . . . . . . . . . . . . . . . . . . . . . . . . . . ."Work hard. Tough it out."

CHARLES R. SWINDOLL
FROM "GROWING STRONG IN THE SEASONS OF LIFE"

# 12 SURE-FIRE WAYS TO RAISE DELINQUENT CHILDREN

### 1.

Begin from infancy to give the child everything he wants. In this way he will grow up to believe the world owes him a living.

### 2.

When he picks up bad words, laugh at him. This will make him think he's cute. It will also encourage him to pick up "cuter" phrases that will blow off the top of your head later.

### 3.

Never give him any spiritual training. Wait till he is twenty-one and then let him "decide for himself."

### 4.

Avoid use of the word "wrong." It may develop a guilt complex. This will condition him to believe that society is against him, and he is being persecuted.

### 5.

Pick up everything he leaves lying around (books, shoes, and clothing). Do everything for him so he will be experienced in throwing all responsibility onto others.

### 6.

Let him read any printed matter he can get his hands on. Be careful that the silverware and drinking glasses are sterilized, but let his mind feast on garbage.

## 7.

Quarrel frequently in the presence of your child. In this way he will not be too shocked when the home is broken up later.

## 8.

Give a child all the spending money he wants. Never let him earn his own. Why should he have things as tough as you had them?

## 9.

Satisfy his every craving for food, drink, and comfort. See that every sensual desire is gratified. Denial of his desires may lead to harmful frustration.

## 10.

Take his part against neighbors, teachers, and policemen. They are all prejudiced against your child.

## 11.

When he gets into real trouble, apologize for yourself by saying, "I never could do anything with him."

## 12.

Prepare for a life of grief.

AUTHOR UNKNOWN

# THE 10 COMMANDMENTS
## OF DISCIPLINE

### 1.
#### EXAMINE THE EVIDENCE

Examine all the evidence and interview all witnesses before bringing charges.

### 2.
#### JUSTICE SHOULD BE SWIFT

Don't make your kids sit on "death row" for hours waiting for a pardon from the governor.

### 3.
#### DON'T DISCIPLINE OUT OF ANGER

Try not to discipline in the heat of the moment, when emotions are peaking. Before you lose control, call a parenting time-out.

### 4.
#### KEEP YOUR WORD

Don't make threats you don't intend to keep. If you warn your child that he will be disciplined the next time he breaks a certain household rule, be sure to follow through.

### 5.
#### DON'T EXHUME THE BODIES OF THE PAST

Stay current. Discipline your children for today's "mess-up," not the one that occurred last week, last month, or even last year.

### 6.
#### NEVER ARGUE WITH YOUR KIDS

Some kids use arguing as a stalling tactic to avoid discipline. They figure if they plead their case vehemently enough, they might get you to reverse your decision.

### 7.
#### PUNISHMENT SHOULD FIT THE CRIME

Don't give your kids the death penalty for a misdemeanor—for instance, if your teenager misses curfew by a few minutes. Any discipline should reflect the severity of the problem.

### 8.
#### HELP YOUR KIDS SEE THEIR ROLE BEFORE YOU DISCIPLINE

Help your kids understand their mistakes and the possible motivation behind the misdeed or misconduct. If an apology is in order be sure they know why and to whom it should be directed. This ends the case by bringing "closure" to their act.

### 9.
#### DON'T WITHHOLD FORGIVENESS—IT BECOMES MANIPULATIVE

Some parents stay mad as a way to remain in a one-up power position over their children. Letting go of your anger and communicating forgiveness helps a child do the right thing next time.

### 10.
#### NEVER DISCIPLINE YOUR CHILDREN FOR AN ACCIDENT

GREG CYNAUMON, PH.D.
CONDENSED FROM "HOW TO AVOID ALIENATING YOUR KIDS IN 10 EASY STEPS"

# THE SIX A'S OF PARENTING

## 1.
### BE AWARE

Study your children. They're wonderful creations. Listen to them, watch them, ask them questions. Talk with them, not to them. Discover their likes and dislikes, their dreams and fears, their strengths and weaknesses. Recognize how special they are.

## 2.
### BE ASSERTIVE

There are lessons you've learned from life, so pass them on. Teach truth. Provide reasonable rules and consistent consequences when those rules are broken. Be strong and give your children security without being rigid, insensitive, abusive, angry, or exasperating.

## 3.
### BE ACCEPTING

Focus on the positives and assist children with their negatives. Don't expect perfection from them, lest they turn and expect it from you. Remember that children are often immature and teenagers are frequently impulsive. Be patient with them.

## 4.
### BE APPROACHABLE

One of the biggest problems is emotional distance from your children. Be close to your children. Spend quality time with them. Laugh with them; play with them; enjoy them. Take them on walks and outings and vacations. Truly connect with them.

## 5.
### BE AFFECTIONATE

Hug them often and tell them you love them every day. Give them compliments and encourage them versus discouraging them. Don't yell, hit, name call, or belittle them. Treat them gently and with respect. Treasure them.

## 6.
### BE ALERT

The world is full of dangers and temptations. As parents we are protectors. Watch over your children and warn them. Protect them without being paranoid. Most importantly of all, pray for them daily.

DR. STEVE STEPHENS
PSYCHOLOGIST AND FATHER OF THREE

# PARENTING 101

### 1.
PAY MORE ATTENTION TO YOUR MARRIAGE—OR YOURSELF,
IF YOU'RE A SINGLE PARENT—THAN YOU DO TO THE CHILDREN.

Your marriage, if it is strong and satisfying, will give your children more security than any amount of attention. If you are single, your sense of self-respect and fulfillment as a person can act as the same sort of anchor for children.

### 2.
EXPECT YOUR CHILDREN TO OBEY.

Don't apologize for decisions you make in their lives. Children need powerful parents upon whom they can count to be authoritative, decisive, and trustworthy. *You* are in charge of the family.

### 3.
NURTURE YOUR CHILDREN'S RESPONSIBILITY WITHIN THIS STRUCTURE.

Allow them to make choices, and let them know that they must accept the outcomes. From an early age, expect them to make regular, tangible contributions to the family. That means chores they don't get paid for. And it means letting your children take responsibility for their own actions.

### 4.
SAY NO AND SAY IT OFTEN.

If the response is a tantrum, so be it. Exposure to frustration prepares children for the realities of adulthood and gives them a tolerance of frustration that eventually develops perseverance—a key ingredient to every success story. Your obligation is not to make your children happy, but to give them the skills to pursue happiness on their own.

## 5.
### WHERE TOYS ARE CONCERNED, LESS IS MORE.

Having too many toys destroys a young child's ability to make creative decisions. If a youngster has too many options, he becomes overwhelmed and can't decide what to play with.

## 6.
### TURN OFF THE TUBE.

Preschool children need to play so they can develop basic competency skills, learned by touching and exploring their environment. Nothing happens when a child sits passively in front of a television screen.

## 7.
### DON'T BE INTIMIDATED BY THE EXPERTS.

Use suggestions and ideas that make sense to you, but remember that all parents make mistakes now and then...and children aren't permanently scarred by it. Raise your children your way and enjoy it.

JOHN ROSEMOND
CONDENSED FROM "BOTTOM LINE PERSONAL"

# 10 THINGS TO DO WHEN CHILDREN ARE AFRAID

### 1.
### BE CLOSE

*Just the presence of someone safe is calming.*

### 2.
### TOUCH THEM

*Holding hands, hugs, rubbing their back and any form of reassuring affection helps.*

### 3.
### SPEAK GENTLY AND CONFIDENTLY

*Your voice is a point of familiarity and safety, so watch your tone.*

### 4.
### LISTEN

*Let them tell you about their fears no matter how irrational. Be attentive and patient. Remember, what they say is very important to them.*

### 5.
### GIVE THEM SOMETHING SPECIFIC TO DO

*Taking action helps children feel like they have some power when overwhelmed.*

### 6.
### GIVE THEM A POSITIVE FOCUS

*When they think of something good or safe or reassuring, fears don't seem so big.*

## 7.
### PRAY WITH THEM

*Seeking God's protection or comfort is something we all need.
Remind them God is always close and he always cares.*

## 8.
### GIVE THEM SOMETHING FAMILIAR

*Familiar objects (such as a blanket, photograph, necklace,
ring, or stuffed animal) help children relax.*

## 9.
### REASSURE THEM THAT THERE IS ALWAYS A WAY OUT

*Teach them how to problem solve and figure out what to do. Come up
with as many solutions as possible. Reassure them that things which
seem very frightening now often don't seem so bad in a year or two.*

## 10.
### REMIND THEM THAT WE ALL HAVE FEARS

*Tell them about what frightened you at their age
and how you handled it.*

DR. STEVE STEPHENS
PSYCHOLOGIST AND FATHER OF THREE

FAMILY VALUES

# JOBS KIDS CAN DO

**FOUR TO SIX-YEAR-OLDS CAN:**

Sort laundry

Dust

Make bed

Set table

Pick up toys

Feed pets

Wipe floors

**SIX TO TEN-YEAR-OLDS CAN:**

Fold clothes

Vacuum

Change bed linens

Clean bathroom

Empty dishwasher

Prepare lunch

Groom pets

Plan & plant garden

Water plants

Pull weeds

| TEN TO THIRTEEN-YEAR-OLDS CAN: | THIRTEEN TO HIGH SCHOOL CAN: |
|---|---|
| Wash, dry, & fold clothes | Wash windows |
| Mow lawn | Paint |
| Rake | Clean oven |
| Wash & dry dishes | Wash walls |
| Wash & vacuum car | Trim hedges |
| Plan & prepare meals | Tutor younger siblings |
| Clean refrigerator | Defrost freezer |
| Shovel snow | Wash & wax floors |
| | Run errands |

DOREEN BUTTON
MOM TO THREE BUSY HOME-SCHOOL KIDS

# WINNING OVER THE PICKY EATER

### 1.
#### SCALE DOWN YOUR EXPECTATIONS

*If your child eats small portions, don't worry.*

### 2.
#### LIMIT AFTERNOON SNACKS

*Don't deprive children of an afternoon snack, but make it small
and nutritious if you expect them to eat a full dinner.
Offer fresh fruit, cheese, or graham crackers.*

### 3.
#### LIMIT DRINKS

*Parents often underestimate how filling fruit juice and milk can be.*

### 4.
#### SERVE SMALL PORTIONS

*Put less on their plate than you think they will eat.
You can always serve seconds.*

### 5.
#### MAKE MEALTIME PLEASANT

*Include children in conversation, and don't make the dinner hour
a time for criticism or arguments.
Don't force your child to remain at the table with a plate of food
after the rest of the family is finished.*

### 6.
#### EXPECT GOOD MANNERS

*Let your child know he or she is to be at the table on time and
to refrain from making faces and rude comments about the food.*

### 7.
#### DON'T BECOME A SHORT-ORDER COOK

*Serve a well-balanced meal, and let your child make choices
from what is prepared.*

### 8.
#### AVOID THE DESSERT DOWNFALL

*Denying a picky eater dessert is another no-win situation.*

### 9.
#### LOOK AT THE BIG PICTURE

*Keep in mind your child's diet over the long haul and not just
at a particular meal. Your responsibility is to provide healthful food
in a happy setting. Children are most likely to develop new tastes when
they are free to discover food on their own without bribery or praise.*

ELLYN SATTER
FROM "HOW TO GET YOUR KID TO EAT...BUT NOT TOO MUCH"

# TABLE MANNERS

REMEMBER—THERE IS A REASON FOR EVERY RULE.

PLACE  no elbows on the table unless all the dishes are removed following the meal.

CHEW  with your mouth closed.

HOLD  the silverware correctly.

CUT  one bit of meat at a time.

PASS  food to the right.

PASS  both the salt and pepper shakers.

SIT  up straight in your chair.

MODIFY  your voice so that only your tablemates can hear you.

EXCUSE  yourself to individuals on each side of you if you must leave the table.

REFUSE  food only if you must by saying kindly, "No, thank you."

SAY,  "Please pass the…"

WATCH to see that all condiments near you are passed around the table.

UNFOLD a large restaurant napkin halfway. Place the fold toward your knees. Leave it in your lap until you leave the table, except when you use the napkin.

EAT at a moderate speed. Don't make others wait for you to finish.

PLACE used silverware on a plate, not on the tablecloth (even during a course).

EAT quietly, making no noise with your mouth or silverware.

REMOVE seeds, pits, gristle, etc. from your mouth with the utensil you used to put it into your mouth. Do not use a cloth napkin. Small bones may be removed with one's thumb and forefinger for safety.

REFUSE beverage by simply saying, "No, thank you." Do not invert the cup or glass. (The wait staff may turn it over.)

JUNE HINES MOORE
MOORE THAN MANNERS CONSULTING

# WHEN TO TEACH
# YOUR CHILD MANNERS

AGE THREE TO FOUR:

Saying "Hello" and "Goodbye"
Saying "Please" and "Thank you"
Shaking hands

AGE FOUR TO SIX:

Saying "Excuse me"
Using a fork and spoon properly
Asking for food to be passed
Using a napkin
Talking without a mouth full of food
Not making a scene in public

AGE SIX TO TWELVE:

Not interrupting others
Saying "Excuse me" when interrupting becomes necessary
Offering help when it is needed
Showing respect for elders
Refraining from making hurtful comments
Responding when spoken to
Respecting property at home and away

Answering the telephone properly
Keeping his or her room clean and picked up
Doing assigned chores cheerfully, punctually, and efficiently
Playing music at a reasonably low decibel level
Respecting the privacy of others
Waiting one's proper turn in line
Saying "Excuse me" when bumping into someone
Attending to one's guest
Writing thank-you notes for gifts, overnight visits, and special treats
    of any kind
Being punctual
Depositing trash in proper receptacle
Observing rules of safety such as walking, biking, skating

JUNE HINES MOORE
FROM "YOU CAN RAISE A WELL-MANNERED CHILD"

FAMILY VALUES

# THE 10 MOST IMPORTANT MANNERS TO TEACH YOUR CHILDREN

### 1.
*Meeting and greeting people properly.*

### 2.
*Being a gracious host and a welcome guest.*

### 3.
*Good mouth manners: "Yes" and "No" (or "Yes, ma'am"and
"No, ma'am," not "Yeah" or a grunt), "hello, goodbye,
thank you, please, excuse me, I'm sorry, may I?"*

### 4.
*Proper conduct for church and other public places.*

### 5.
*Writing, coloring, or drawing thank-you notes.*

### 6.
*Properly responding to invitations and following through on the response.*

### 7.
*Good (not perfect) table manners.*

### 8.
*Proper telephone talk.*

### 9.
*Showing deference to elders and authority figures.*

### 10.
*Opening doors for others.*

JUNE HINES MOORE
FROM "YOU CAN RAISE A WELL-MANNERED CHILD"

# FAMILY LOVE

*Bonding together*

13

# LOVING YOUR KIDS

Take time with your children.

Set your children a good example.

Give your children ideals for living.

Have a lot of activities planned.

Discipline your children.

Teach them about God.

BILLY GRAHAM
FROM "GOD'S LITTLE INSTRUCTION BOOK FOR DAD"

# TODAY'S KIDS DESPERATELY NEED HEROES WHO...

...play catch, enjoy tea parties, or wrestle because the heart of a child is there and they set out to capture it.

...laugh till their belly hurts and tears fall from their eyes while secretly creating deep friendships and memories that last a lifetime.

...make mistakes but consider them to be wonderful opportunities to learn.

...place an out-of-tune preschool concert or a ten-year-old's baseball game on life's agenda because they are of infinite worth to those playing.

...love at all times, because love is a gift freely given and not a reward for service well done.

...listen eye to eye and with both ears even if it means getting on one knee.

...admit when they are wrong and work to make things right.

...hear about those in need and say, "Let's do something to help right now!" and set off an uncontrollable wildfire of generosity and kindness.

...give the credit to others and empower those they touch to succeed in all that they do.

...model love as action, commitment, and truth even when it hurts because they believe God can work miracles in even the hardest heart.

...love the Lord with all their heart, soul, and mind and know that the rest is just details.

MARTY WILKINS
DAD OF THREE, HIGH SCHOOL TEACHER AND COACH

# BLESSED ARE PARENTS WHO...

### 1.
Blessed are parents who listen to their children, for they in turn will be heard.

### 2.
Blessed are they who do not expect more of their children than is appropriate for their level of maturity, for they shall not be disappointed.

### 3.
Blessed are parents who do not attempt to tackle the new math, for they shall not fail.

### 4.
Blessed are parents who can laugh at themselves, for their children will laugh with them and not at them.

### 5.
Blessed are the parents who may be called "old-fashioned." They can be assured they are on the right track, for so have children persecuted parents for generations, and their opinions will change by the time they are old enough to pay taxes.

### 6.
Blessed are they who teach their children to understand and love each other, for they shall not get caught in the crossfire of a sibling war.

### 7.
Blessed are the parents who let their children do for themselves what they are capable of doing, for they shall not be merely unpaid servants.

### 8.
Blessed are the parents who take their children with them often, for they shall see the world with fresh eyes.

### 9.
Blessed are the parents who have found success-outlets for their energies, for they will not need their children as status symbols or as justifications.

### 10.
Blessed are the parents who do not pretend to be perfect, for their children will not be disillusioned.

ASSOCIATION FOR CHILDREN AND ADULTS WITH LEARNING DISABILITIES (ACLD)
PITTSBURGH, PENNSYLVANIA

# A CHILD'S 10 COMMANDMENTS
# TO PARENTS

### COMMANDMENT 1:

My hands are small; please don't expect perfection whenever I make a bed, draw a picture, or throw a ball. My legs are short; please slow down so that I can keep up with you.

### COMMANDMENT 2:

My eyes have not seen the world as yours have; please let me explore safely. Don't restrict me unnecessarily.

### COMMANDMENT 3:

Housework will always be there. I'm only little for such a short time—please take time to explain things to me about this wonderful world, and do so willingly.

### COMMANDMENT 4:

My feelings are tender; please be sensitive to my needs. Don't nag me all day long. (You wouldn't want to be nagged for your inquisitiveness.) Treat me as you would like to be treated.

### COMMANDMENT 5:

I am a special gift from God; please treasure me as God intended you to do, holding me accountable for my actions, giving me guidelines to live by, and disciplining me in a loving manner.

### COMMANDMENT 6:

I need your encouragement to grow. Please go easy on the criticism; remember, you can criticize the things I do without criticizing me.

### COMMANDMENT 7:

Please give me the freedom to make decisions concerning myself. Permit me to fail, so that I can learn from my mistakes. Then someday I'll be prepared to make the kinds of decisions life requires of me.

### COMMANDMENT 8:

Please don't do things over for me. Somehow that makes me feel that my efforts didn't quite measure up to your expectations. I know it's hard, but please don't try to compare me with my brother or my sister.

### COMMANDMENT 9:

Please don't be afraid to leave for a weekend together. Kids need vacations from parents, just as parents need vacations from kids. Besides, it's a great way to show us kids that your marriage is very special.

### COMMANDMENT 10:

Please take me to Sunday school and church regularly, setting a good example for me to follow. I enjoy learning more about God.

DR. KEVIN LEMAN
FROM "GETTING THE BEST OUT OF YOUR KIDS"

# MEANINGFUL TOUCH

*Hold hands during mealtime prayers.*

*Walk, one-on-one, with each child. Swing hands and talk.
Tell jokes. Sing.*

*Bad day? Sigh dramatically and say,
"I sure could use a great big hug from someone special."*

*Wonderful day? Shout, "Hey, everybody!
Come hug me! I had the best day!"*

*Make "Hug Sandwiches."
With your spouse, gently surprise unsuspecting children.*

*Declare "100 Hugs Day." Count.*

*Do Four-Direction Kisses: north (foreheads),
south (chins), east/west (cheeks).*

*Wrap your arm around your children during church,
while waiting together, or watching TV.*

*Apply The Pat Principle: "When in doubt, pat."
God made lots of patting places—heads, cheeks, knees,
hands, shoulders, backs.*

LORRI CARDWELL-CASEY
FROM "HOMELIFE" MAGAZINE

# 50 WAYS TO LOVE YOUR CHILDREN

1. Hug every morning. 2. Go to zoos, parades, and amusement parks. 3. Hang their art and awards on the refrigerator. 4. Create family traditions. 5. Be patient. 6. Apologize when grumpy. 7. Go camping. 8. Play tic-tac-toe and hide-and-seek. 9. Always carry Band-Aids and gumdrops. 10. Know their strengths. 11. Compliment them. 12. Encourage them. 13. Appreciate them. 14. Eat meals together. 15. Slow down. 16. Respect their privacy. 17. Listen. 18. Don't discipline in anger. 19. Be consistent. 20. Say "I love you" frequently. 21. Let them be silly. 22. Accept imperfections. 23. Reward good behavior. 24. Explain the rules clearly. 25. Laugh often. 26. Go to their favorite restaurant. 27. Invite their friends over. 28. Buy ice cream cones. 29. Go on vacations. 30. Know when to be gentle and when to be firm. 31. Make birthdays unforgettable. 32. Teach responsibility and respect. 33. Choose your battles. 34. Don't embarrass them. 35. Help with schoolwork. 36. Protect them. 37. Build memories. 38. Keep promises. 39. Say "no" when needed. 40. Don't yell. 41. Give gifts. 42. Model virtues. 43. Pray with them. 44. Pray for them. 45. Talk with their teachers. 46. Tell them you're proud of them. 47. Reach out. 48. Count stars together. 49. Talk every bedtime. 50. Let go with a blessing.

DR. STEVE STEPHENS
FROM "STORIES FOR THE FAMILY'S HEART"

# WORDS FOR YOUR FAMILY

*I'm proud of you.*

*Way to go!*

*Bingo! You did it.*

*Magnificent.*

*I knew you could do it.*

*What a good helper.*

*You're very special to me.*

*I trust you.*

*What a treasure.*

*Hooray for you!*

*Beautiful work.*

*You're a real trooper.*

*Well done.*

*That's so creative.*

*You make my day.*

*You're a joy.*

*Give me a big hug.*

*You're such a good listener.*

*You figured it out.*

*I love you.*

*You're so responsible.*

*You remembered.*

*You're the best.*

*You sure tried hard.*

*I've got to hand it to you.*

*I couldn't be prouder of you.*

*You light up my day.*

*My buttons are popping off.*

*I'm praying for you.*

*You're wonderful.*

*I'm behind you.*

GARY SMALLEY AND JOHN TRENT
FROM "LEAVING THE LIGHT ON"

FAMILY LOVE

# 18 MEMOS FROM YOUR CHILD

### 1.

Don't spoil me. I know quite well that I ought not to have all I ask for. I'm testing you.

### 2.

Don't be afraid to be firm with me. I prefer it; it makes me feel more secure.

### 3.

Don't let me form bad habits. I have to rely on you to detect them in the early stages.

### 4.

Don't make me feel smaller than I am. It only makes me behave stupidly big.

### 5.

Don't correct me in front of people if you can help it. I'll take much more notice if you talk quietly with me in private.

### 6.

Don't protect me from consequences. I need to learn the painful way sometimes.

### 7.

Don't be too upset when I say "I hate you." It isn't you I hate, but your power to thwart me.

### 8.

Don't take too much notice of my small ailments. Sometimes they get me the attention I need.

### 9.

Don't nag. If you do, I shall have to protect myself by appearing deaf.

### 10.

Don't make rash promises. Remember that I feel badly let down when promises are broken.

## 11.

Don't forget that I cannot explain myself as well as I should like. That is why I'm not always very accurate.

## 12.

Don't be inconsistent. That completely confuses me and makes me lose faith in you.

## 13.

Don't tell me my fears are silly. They are terribly real and you can do much to reassure me if you try to understand.

## 14.

Don't put me off when I ask questions. If you do you will find that I stop asking and seek my information elsewhere.

## 15.

Don't ever suggest that you are perfect or infallible. It gives me too great a shock when I discover you are neither.

## 16.

Don't ever think it is beneath your dignity to apologize to me. An honest apology makes me feel surprisingly warm toward you.

## 17.

Don't forget how quickly I am growing up. It must be very difficult for you to keep pace with me, but please try.

## 18.

Don't forget I need lots of understanding and love.

AUTHOR UNKNOWN

FAMILY LOVE

# 10 IDEAS FOR MAKING A
# MEMORABLE MOTHER'S DAY

### 1.
*Have a florist deliver a corsage and
on the card tell her you're taking her to dinner.*

### 2.
*Create a May-to-May calendar using family pictures.
Place a star on a day each month for a special date you will have with her.*

### 3.
*Gather scrapbook supplies and spend the day working on it together.*

### 4.
*Plant some colorful summer flowers in her yard and/or patio pots.*

### 5.
*Have each family member write a special memory they have of her.
Tuck each note in a separate Mother's Day card
selected or created by each individual.*

### 6.
*Prepare a picnic lunch and let her pick the place it will be enjoyed.*

### 7.
*Have the family gather around her and ask her to share
favorite memories of her childhood.
Be sure to have a video or tape recorder going.*

### 8.
*Give her a basket full of things that help her relax.*
*Include a long, narrow tablet and ask her to list things*
*she's been wishing help with. Recruit family members*
*to get the jobs done in the next few weeks.*

### 9.
*Give the gift of your time by helping her sort through pictures*
*and bring her photo album up-to-date.*

### 10.
*Remember to tell her how much you love her*
*and what you love about her.*

MARILYN MCAULEY
MOTHER OF THREE, GRANDMOTHER OF SIX

# 10 IDEAS FOR A FABULOUS, UNFORGETTABLE FATHER'S DAY

## 1.

If you can't be together, mark your calendar so you will be sure to call your father. Include comments about what he means to you as a father, mentor, and friend.

## 2.

Pick a photo of you and your father together and write a note to him about why the picture is meaningful to you. Send it in time to arrive a day before Father's Day.

## 3.

Buy tickets to a game of his favorite sport and go together.

## 4.

Offer to join him at his church for the Father's Day services.

## 5.

Write him a letter thanking him for two or more traits he taught you that really make you a more successful adult.

## 6.

Record a cassette for him that shares a special memory of childhood that you both cherish so he can enjoy it in the car or at home.

## 7.

Order a beef stick and cheese box, or some other favorite snack gift package, and have it delivered a day early. Enclose a card that says you will join him to watch a game or movie of his choice.

### 8.

Make a video for him of your childhood home and include a commentary on memories and lessons you really value from your childhood.

### 9.

Take him to a dinner place of his choice and surprise him with two or three of his friends that he may not see often. Plan this for the day before or after Father's Day so they will be available.

### 10.

Ask your brothers and sisters to join you in writing notes sharing how your father's influence and availability over the years has benefited your family life. Include them in a memory book with a nice masculine cover.

DANIEL L. MCAULEY
FATHER OF THREE, GRANDFATHER OF SIX

FAMILY LOVE

# WHAT KIDS APPRECIATE

**1.**
We were often spontaneously getting hugged even apart from completing a task or chore.

**2.**
They would let me explain my side of the story.

**3.**
They would take each of us out individually for a special breakfast with Mom and Dad.

**4.**
My mother always carried pictures of each of us in her purse.

**5.**
They would watch their tone of voice when they argued.

**6.**
My parents made sure that each one of us kids appeared in the family photos.

**7.**
They were willing to admit when they were wrong and say "I'm sorry."

**8.**
I saw my parents praying for me even when I didn't feel I deserved it.

**9.**
My folks wrote up a special "story of my birth" that they read to me every year.

**10.**
They attended all of my open houses at school.

**11.**
My mother and father would ask us children our opinions on important family decisions.

**12.**
My mom had a great sense of humor, but she never made us kids the brunt of her jokes.

**13.**
My parents wouldn't change things in my bedroom without asking me if it was okay with me.

**14.**
When I wrecked my parents' car, my father's first reaction was to hug me and let me cry instead of yelling at me.

### 15.

My parents were patient with me when I went through my long-hair stage in high school.

### 16.

My mother would pray with me about important decisions I was facing, or even that I would have a good day at school.

### 17.

We would have "family meetings" every two weeks where everyone would share their goals and problems.

### 18.

Even though I didn't like it at the time, the chores my parents made me do helped me learn responsibility.

### 19.

When I was down about my boyfriend breaking up with me, my father took extra time just to listen to me and cry with me.

### 20.

My parents never acted like they were perfect, and they never expected us to be perfect either.

### 21.

My mother would let me explain my point of view on issues—even when she disagreed with me. She always made me feel that my opinion was important.

### 22.

My parents didn't compare my abilities with those of my older brother or the other kids at school, but helped me see my own unique value.

GARY SMALLEY AND JOHN TRENT
SELECTED FROM A LIST OF ONE HUNDRED, FROM "THE BLESSING"

# LONG-DISTANCE GRANDPARENTING

Call your grandchild regularly.
Keep up with your grandchild's interests and
activities and talk about them when you phone.

If you have access to a video recorder,
your grandchildren will love
a videotape of you reading a bedtime story.
Mail the tape and the book.

Cut out newspaper comic strips.
White out the words and write in your own.
Mail them to your grandchild.
Children love to receive mail addressed to them.

Send inexpensive gifts—a bookmark or stickers
on a day other than a birthday or holiday;
a little something that says "I love you."

As your grandchild learns to read, write an
original story of three or four paragraphs,
glue it to colored paper and mail it.

Take your grandchild's address with you
when you travel and send postcards.

Write letters about even simple things that happen at
your house: squirrels stashing their food under the
tree stump or birds singing in the feeder.
Ask simple questions and enclose self-addressed
stamped envelopes for the answers.

Send audio tapes telling your grandchild
what is happening at your house. Listening to the
tape makes the child feel part of your everyday
life. Tapes laced with expressions of love for the
child will reinforce feelings for you.

Know what interests your grandchild who's
in high school. If it's sports, be up on his or her
favorite team when they play.

Weave your faith in God into letters
and phone calls in a loving, honest way.

IRENE ENDICOTT
FROM "GRANDPARENTING BY GRACE"

# TAKE THE TIME

**1.**
For parents of more than one child, choose one activity in
each child's school that you will be involved in.

**2.**
Help your child choose at least one sport or group
activity outside of school to be involved in.

**3.**
Choose one way in which your family can help the community,
and talk about why community service is important.

**4.**
Read to or with your child every day, even if it's only for ten minutes.

**5.**
Include your children in some decisions about family activities, and work
together to create a family calendar to record what you decide.

**6.**
Choose one fun activity that the whole family can do together—
play music or softball, or plant a garden, bike, or cook together.

**7.**
Start a family scrapbook and ask everyone to add something
to it each month.

**8.**
Ask your children to think of three ways to
make your neighborhood safer, and then work on it together.

THE SEARCH INSTITUTE

# WISDOM

## 14

*Learning from the experience of others*

# WISE THINGS YOUR GRANDMA TOLD YOU

You are special.

Manners matter.

Treat others the way you want to be treated.

Your life can be what you want it to be.

Take the days one day at a time.

Always play fair.

Count your blessings, not your troubles.

Don't put limits on yourself.

It's never too late.

Put things back where you found them.

Decisions are too important to leave to chance.

Reach for the stars.

Clean up after yourself.

Nothing wastes more energy than worrying.

The longer you carry a problem, the heavier it gets.

Say "I'm sorry" when you've hurt someone.

A little love goes a long way.

Friendship is always a good investment.

Don't take things too seriously.

PATTI MACGREGOR
FROM "FAMILY TIMES: GROWING TOGETHER IN FUN AND FAITH"

# TRUE UNDERSTANDING

WE DO NOT UNDERSTAND:

Joy...until we face sorrow.

Faith...until it is tested.

Peace...until faced with conflict.

Trust...until we are betrayed.

Love...until it is lost.

Hope...until confronted with doubts.

AUTHOR UNKNOWN

# A SHORT COURSE
# IN HUMAN RELATIONS

The six most important words: "I admit I made a mistake."

The five most important words: "You did a good job."

The four most important words: "What is your opinion?"

The three most important words: "If you please."

The two most important words: "Thank you."

The one most important word: "We."

The least important word: "I"

AUTHOR UNKNOWN
AS CITED IN "MORE OF... THE BEST OF BITS & PIECES," ROB GILBERT, PH.D. ED.

# RULES FOR LIVING

*If you open it, close it.*

*If you turn it on, turn it off.*

*If you unlock it, lock it up.*

*If you break it, admit it.*

*If you can't fix it, call in someone who can.*

*If you borrow it, return it.*

*If you value it, take care of it.*

*If you make a mess, clean it up.*

*If you move it, put it back.*

*If it belongs to someone else and you want to use it, get permission.*

*If you don't know how to operate it, leave it alone.*

*If it's none of your business, don't ask questions.*

*If it ain't broke, don't fix it.*

*If it will brighten someone's day, say it.*

*If it will tarnish someone's reputation, keep it to yourself.*

AUTHOR UNKNOWN

# PLANTING

If you plant for days
—plant flowers

If you plant for years
—plant trees

If you plant for eternity
—plant people

AUTHOR UNKNOWN

# THINK WITH DISCERNMENT

He who knows not,
and knows not that he knows not,
is a fool;
shun him.

He who knows not,
and knows that he knows not,
is a child;
teach him.

He who knows,
and knows not that he knows,
is asleep;
wake him.

He who knows,
and knows that he knows,
is wise;
follow him.

PERSIAN PROVERB

# RESPONSIBILITY

### 1.
*Never put off till tomorrow what you can do today.*

### 2.
*Never trouble another for what you can do yourself.*

### 3.
*Never spend your money before you have it.*

### 4.
*Never buy what you do not want because it is cheap.*

### 5.
*Pride costs us more than hunger, thirst, and cold.*

### 6.
*We never repent of having eaten too little.*

### 7.
*Nothing is troublesome that we do willingly.*

### 8.
*How much pain have cost us the evils which have never happened.*

### 9.
*Take things always by their smooth handle.*

### 10.
*When angry, count to ten before you speak; if very angry, a hundred.*

THOMAS JEFFERSON
THIRD PRESIDENT OF THE UNITED STATES

# WISE SAYINGS FROM THE
# BOOK OF PROVERBS

### 1.
Wise men store up knowledge.
But with the mouth of the foolish, ruin is at hand (10:14).

### 2.
When there are many words, transgression is unavoidable.
But he who restrains his lips is wise (10:19).

### 3.
He who goes about as a talebearer reveals secrets.
But he who is trustworthy conceals a matter (11:13).

### 4.
The one who guards his mouth preserves his life.
The one who opens wide his lips comes to ruin (13:3).

### 5.

He who goes about as a slanderer reveals secrets,
Therefore do not associate with a gossip (20:19).

### 6.

Like a bad tooth and an unsteady foot.
Is confidence in a faithless man in time of trouble (25:19).

### 7.

Like a city that is broken into and without walls.
Is a man who has no control over his spirit (25:28).

CHARLES R. SWINDOLL
FROM "COME BEFORE WINTER"

# WISE SAYINGS FROM
# POOR RICHARD'S ALMANAC

### 1.
*To lengthen thy life, lessen thy meals.*

### 2.
*He that lies down with dogs shall rise up with fleas.*

### 3.
*Better slip with foot than tongue.*

### 4.
*Teach your child to hold his tongue; he'll learn fast enough to speak.*

### 5.
*Humility makes great men twice honorable.*

### 6.
*Tis easy to see, hard to foresee.*

### 7.
*Creditors have better memories than debtors.*

### 8.
*God heals, and the doctor takes the fees.*

## 9.
*No better relation than a prudent and faithful friend.*

## 10.
*Sell not virtue to purchase wealth, nor liberty to purchase power.*

## 11.
*Keep your eyes wide open before marriage, half shut afterward.*

## 12.
*Wish not so much to live long as to live well.*

## 13.
*He that sows thorns should not go barefoot.*

## 14.
*There are three things extremely hard: steel,
a diamond, and to know one's self.*

## 15.
*Success has ruin'd many a man.*

BENJAMIN FRANKLIN
STATESMAN, INVENTOR, AND SCIENTIST

# WHEN SOMETHING RIGHT
# CAN GO WRONG

## 1.

*When in our determination to be bold we become brazen*

## 2.

*When in our desire to be frank we become rude*

## 3.

*When in our effort to be watchful we become suspicious*

## 4.

*When we seek to be serious and become somber*

## 5.

*When we mean to be conscientious and become overscrupulous*

A. W. TOZER
FROM "THE QUOTABLE TOZER"

# SEVEN THINGS GOD HATES

1.

*Haughty eyes*

2.

*A lying tongue*

3.

*Hands that shed innocent blood*

4.

*A heart that devises wicked schemes*

5.

*Feet that are quick to rush into evil*

6.

*A false witness who pours out lies*

7.

*A man who stirs up dissension among brothers.*

KING SOLOMON
FROM PROVERBS 6:16–19 (NIV)

# KNOWING YOURSELF

1.

*What we want most.*

2.

*What we think about most.*

3.

*How we use our money.*

4.

*What we do with our leisure time.*

5.

*The company we enjoy.*

6.

*Whom and what we admire.*

7.

*What we laugh at.*

A. W. TOZER
FROM "THE QUOTABLE TOZER"

# SIX DESTRUCTIVE MISTAKES

### 1.
*The delusion that personal gain is made by crushing others*

### 2.
*The tendency to worry about things*
*that cannot be changed or corrected*

### 3.
*Insisting that a thing is impossible because we cannot accomplish it*

### 4.
*Refusing to set aside trivial preferences*

### 5.
*Neglecting development and refinement of the mind, and*
*not acquiring the habit of reading and studying*

### 6.
*Attempting to compel others to believe and live as we do*

MARCUS TULLIUS CICERO
STATESMAN, PHILOSOPHER, AND ORATOR

# LOVE...

Is very patient
Is kind
Is never jealous
Is never envious
Is never boastful
Is never proud
Is never haughty
Is never selfish
Is never rude
Does not demand its own way
Is not irritable or touchy
Does not hold grudges
Will hardly even notice when others do it wrong
Is never glad about injustice
Rejoices whenever truth wins out
Is loyal no matter what the cost
Will always believe
Will always expect the best
Will always defend
Goes on forever

ST. PAUL THE APOSTLE
CONDENSED FROM 1 CORINTHIANS 13:4–8

# HOPE...

HOPE looks for the good in people instead of harping
on the worst in them.

HOPE opens doors where despair closes them.

HOPE discovers what can be done instead of
grumbling about what cannot be done.

HOPE draws its power from a deep trust in God
and the basic goodness of mankind.

HOPE "lights a candle" instead of "cursing the darkness."

HOPE regards problems, small or large, as opportunities.

HOPE cherishes no illusions, nor does it yield to cynicism.

AUTHOR UNKNOWN

# MORE INSPIRING BOOKS FROM ALICE GRAY & JOHN VAN DIEST

### Stories for a Woman's Heart
COMPILED BY ALICE GRAY
Find a quiet corner and snuggle up with this
enchanting collection of tender stories that celebrate
the wondrous ways of women. These are timeless treasures selected to inspire your
thoughts, stir your soul, and tug at your heart. ISBN 1-57673-474-9

### Stories for a Man's Heart COMPILED BY ALICE GRAY
Encouraging. Inspirational. Humorous. Here is a collection of captivating stories destined to invigorate the hearts of men. Written by many of today's most popular communicators, these stories provide new motivation to be all you can be for those who mean the most to you. ISBN 1-57673-479-X

### Unsolved Miracles COMPILED BY JOHN VAN DIEST
This extraordinary collection of stories shows inspiring and tender answers to prayer and incredible events that can only be explained as miracles of God. Contributions from popular Christian authors reveal God's wondrous and endearing love. ISBN 1-57673-226-6

*Delight yourself in the LORD and He will give you
the desires of your heart.*
PSALM 37:4, NIV

# WE LOVE LISTS!

If you have a favorite list and would like to have it considered for the next edition of *Lists to Live By*, please send it to us.

If you found the list in a magazine or book, please include information about the source (book or magazine title, author, publisher, page number, and date of publication).

If you have written the list, please tell us who you are and what you do.

If you send a list, we will not be able to acknowledge receipt of your list but promise to contact you if we choose to include it in the next book. It is not necessary to send a self-address stamped envelope, but be sure to include your name and address.

Send lists to:

Lists
8800 SE Sunnyside Road
Suite 102-N
Clackamas, OR 97015

# ACKNOWLEDGMENTS

*More than a thousand books and magazines were researched and dozens of professionals interviewed for this collection. A diligent effort has been made to attribute original ownership of each list, and when necessary, obtain permission to reprint. If we have overlooked giving proper credit to anyone, please accept our apologies. If you will contact Multnomah Publishers, Inc., Post Office Box 1720, Sisters, Oregon 97759, with written documentation, corrections will be made prior to additional printings.*

*Notes and acknowledgments are shown in the order the lists appear in each section of the book. For permission to reprint a list, please request permission from the original source shown in the following bibliography. The editors gratefully acknowledge authors, publishers, and agents who granted permission for reprinting these lists.*

## SUCCESS

"Three Secrets to Success" by Sally Ride, astronaut. Source unknown.

"Five Reasons It's Easier to Succeed" by Cathy S. Truett from *It's Easier to Succeed Than to Fail* by Cathy S. Truett. Used by permission of Thomas Nelson, Inc., Nashville, TN, ©1989.

"Six Ways to Bury a Good Idea" as cited in *More of...The Best of Bits & Pieces,* Rob Gilbert, Ph.D., editor. © 1997 by The Economics Press, Inc., 12 Daniel Road, Fairfield, NJ 07004-2565; Phone: 800-526-2554 (US/Canada) or (+1 973) 227-1224 (worldwide). FAX: 973-227-9742 (US/Canada) or (+1 973) 227-9742 (worldwide). E-mail: *info@epinc.com.* Web site: *www.epinc.com.* Please contact The Economics Press, Inc., directly to purchase this book or for subscription information.

"Taking Control of Your Time" by Louise A. Ferrebee, Associate Editor, taken from "Squeezed for Time," *Marriage Partnership* magazine, Summer 1998.

"25 Traits of Entrepreneurs" by Earl Nightingale, co-founder Nightingale Conant, today the largest publisher of audio self-improvement programs in the world. For a catalog, call 1-800-525-9000.

"How to Give Constructive Criticism" by Glenda Hotton, MA DCD LMFT, family counselor in private practice, Valencia, California, specializing in chemical dependency, crisis, and trauma.

"Why We Procrastinate" taken from *The 15-Minute Money Manager* by Bob and Emilie Barnes. © 1993 by Harvest House Publishers, Eugene, Oregon 97402. Used by permission.

"Eight Things You Need to Know about Failure" by Dale Galloway from *How to Feel Like a Somebody Again!* © 1978 by Harvest House Publishers, Eugene, Oregon 97402. Used by permission of the author.

"Commonly Asked Interview Questions" excerpted from *About...Getting Your First Job,* one of the *Life Advice®* pamphlets produced by MetLife's Consumer Education Center (© 1996 by the Metropolitan Life Insurance Company, New York, NY). Used by permission. All rights reserved. To order a free copy of this booklet or any of the over eighty *Life Advice®* pamphlets, call 1-800-METLIFE or visit their web site at *www.metlife.com.*

"What to Include on a Resume" excerpted from *About...Getting Your First Job,* a *Life Advice®* pamphlet produced by MetLife's Consumer Education Center. See above for detailed information.

"Top 10 List for Interviewees" by Lani Williams, Director of Advancement, Western Seminary,

Portland, OR.

"10 Qualities of Successful Bosses" by June Hines Moore, author of *You Can Raise a Well-Mannered Child* and *The Etiquette Advantage,* published by Broadman & Holman, 127 Ninth Ave. N., Nashville, TN 37234. E-mail: *manners@artistotle.net.* Used by permission of Broadman & Holman and the author.

"12 Qualities of Successful Employees" by June Hines Moore. Used by permission of Broadman & Holman and the author.

"14 Ways to Shock Your Boss" by David Sanford, freelance writer. David Sanford is a lay pastor and senior director of publishing for the Luis Palau Evangelistic Association in Portland, Oregon. Used by permission.

"12 Steps to Creative Thinking" by James Lund, Marketing Copy Editor. Used by permission of author.

"How to Become a Lifelong Learner" by Bill Mowry from "Lifelong Learning," *Discipleship Journal,* May/June 1998. Bill Mowry provides leadership to Creation Resources, a Navigator ministry committed to helping people become ministry innovators and lifelong learners.

"Your Future Depends On..." taken from *The 15-Minute Money Manager* by Bob and Emilie Barnes. © 1993 by Harvest House Publishers, Eugene, Oregon 97402. Used by permission.

"What Is Success?" by Ralph Waldo Emerson (1803-1882).

# FRIENDSHIP

"Hints for a Happy Friendship" by Bruce and Cheryl Bickel and Stan and Karin Jantz from *Life's Little Handbook of Wisdom,* published by Barbour Publishing, P.O. Box 719, Uhlrichsville, Ohio, 44683, ©1992. Used by permission.

"How to Get Along with People" by Norman Vincent Peale from *Help Yourself With God's Help* booklet. Used by permission of the Peale Center, Pawling, NY.

"Celebrate Your Differences" by Dr. Steve Stephens from *Marriage: Experience the Best,* published by Vision House Publishing, Gresham, OR, ©1996. Used by permission of the author.

"Rating Yourself as a Friend" from *In the Company of Friends* by Brenda Hunter and Holly Larson, Multnomah Publishers, Inc., Sisters, OR, © 1996. Used by permission.

"To Be a Good Friend" taken from *Friends Through Thick and Thin* by Gloria Gaither, Sue Buchanan, Peggy Benson, and Joy MacKenzie. © 1998 by The Zondervan Corporation. Used by permission of Zondervan Publishing House.

"Watch What You Say" from *God Came Near* by Max Lucado, Multnomah Publishers, Inc., Sisters, OR, © 1987. Used by permission.

"How to Forgive and Forget" excerpted from *Forgive And Forget* by Lewis B. Smedes. © 1984 by Lewis B. Smedes. Reprinted by permission of HarperCollins Publishers, Inc.

"12 Times to Say 'I'm Sorry'" by Dr. Steve Stephens, Clackamas, Oregon. Used by permission of the author.

"Mending a Friendship" by Alan Loy McGinnis. Reprinted from *The Friendship Factor* by Alan Loy McGinnis, © 1979 Augsburg Publishing House, Minneapolis, MN. Used by permission of Augsburg Fortress.

"If You're Going to Fight..." from *Somehow Inside Eternity: Thoughts to Last an Eternity* by Dr. Richard

C. Halverson, Multnomah Publishers, Inc., Sisters, OR, ©1980. Used by permission.

"How to Build a Friendship with Someone You're Dating" by Dick Purnell. This article was taken from *Decision* magazine, February, 1998; © 1998 Billy Graham Evangelistic Association, used by permission, all rights reserved.

"Finding a Listening Ear" by Janis Long Harris from *Marriage Partnership* magazine, Winter 1997. Used by permission of the author.

"Keeping a Confidence" by Joanna Wallace and Deanna Wallace from *Especially for a Woman* by Joanna Wallace and Deanna Wallace. Used by permission of Thomas Nelson, Inc., Nashville, TN, © 1994.

"10 Ways to Welcome a New Neighbor" by Barbara Baumgardner, freelance writer, Bend, Oregon. Used by permission of the author.

"Nurturing Long-Distance Friendships" by Renée Sanford. Renée Sanford is a freelance writer living in Portland, Oregon. Married with four children; her best friend lives in Europe.

"What Is Love?" by Father James Keller, founder, The Christophers, as cited in *More of…The Best of Bits & Pieces,* Rob Gilbert, Ph.D., editor. © 1997 by The Economics Press, Inc.

## VIRTUE

"Destiny" by Frank Outlaw, as cited in *More of…The Best of Bits & Pieces,* Rob Gilbert, Ph.D., editor. © 1997 by The Economics Press, Inc.

"20 Gifts to Give" by Charles R. Swindoll from *The Finishing Touch,* Charles R. Swindoll, © 1994, Word Publishing, Nashville, Tennessee. All rights reserved.

"Actions That Take Courage" by Dr. Steve Stephens, Clackamas, Oregon. Used by permission of the author.

"Benjamin Franklin's 13 Virtues" from *The Autobiography and Other Writings by Benjamin Franklin,* Peter Shaw, editor, Bantam Books, NY ©1982.

"What I Believe In and Value" from *Getting the Right Things Right* by Charlie Hedges, Multnomah Publishers, Inc., Sisters, OR, ©1996. Used by permission of the author.

"People with Character" from *A Diamond in the Rough* compiled by Andrew Stanley. Used by permission of Thomas Nelson, Inc., Nashville, TN, ©1997.

"10 Reasons for Going to Church" by Theodore Roosevelt, condensed from the Ladies' Home Journal, 1917.

"Extreme Virtues" by Ashley Cooper, American columnist, quoted from *More of…The Best of Bits & Pieces.*

"The Adventure of Giving" by Becky Brodin, Minneapolis, MN. Condensed from *Discipleship Journal,* Issue 88, 1995. Used by permission of the author.

"Kindness" by Mother Teresa.

"Rules for Christian Living" by John Wesley.

"Moral Guidance for Your Family" by Mary Ann Kuharski, Minneapolis, MN. Condensed from *HomeLife* magazine, April 1997. Used by permission of the author.

"The 10 Commandments" from *The Holy Bible,* New Living Translation (NLT) © 1996. Used by permission of Tyndale House Publishers, Inc. All rights reserved.

## LIFE'S TRANSITIONS

"Things to Feel Nostalgic About" taken from *Growing Strong in the Seasons of Life* by Charles R. Swindoll. ©1983, The Zondervan Corporation. Used by permission of Zondervan Publishing House.

"Don't Let Your New Baby Drive You Apart" by Rob Parsons from *The 60-Minute Marriage Builder* published by Broadman & Holman, Nashville, TN, ©1998. Used by permission.

"Countdown to College" by Kathy Chapman Sharp and Rebekah D. Sharp from *HomeLife* magazine, July 1997. Used by permission of the authors.

"When Your Adult Children Want to Move Back Home" by Florence Littauer, adapted from *Wake Up, Women!* (Word Publishing). Florence is an author of twenty-seven books and is best known for her book, *Personality Plus,* which has sold a million copies and is translated into eighteen languages. Used by permission of the author.

"Preparing for Retirement" by Alice Gray, Dr. Steve Stephens, and John Van Diest. Used by permission of the authors.

"Four Ways to Grow Old Gracefully" by Abigail Van Buren from *The Oregonian,* July 4, 1998.

"Stay Young While Growing Old" by Tress Van Diest. Used by permission of the author.

"Tough Questions to Ask Elderly Parents" by The Financial Literacy Center, from *New Man* magazine, March/April 1998. Used by permission.

"How Adult Children Can Help Their Parents" by David O. Moberg. Taken from *Decision* magazine, May, 1998; © 1998 Billy Graham Evangelistic Association, used by permission, all rights reserved.

"Questions Parents Should Ask before Moving in with Their Children" by The Mayo Foundation from Mayo Clinic Health Letter, Vol. 9, Dec. 1991 and *A Better Tomorrow* magazine, Nov./Dec. 1994. Used by permission.

"Nursing Home Checklist" by Dan Grady, Chaplain for Nursing Home Ministries. Used by permission of the author.

"A Road Map through Grief" excerpted from *Harsh Grief, Gentle Hope* by Mary White. Used by permission of NavPress, Colorado Springs, CO, ©1995. All rights reserved.

"Recovery from Grief" by Sister Teresa McIntier from *Hospice of Bend Grief Manual.* Used by permission.

"Heaven Is a Place…" by Jay Carty from *Playing the Odds,* published by Vision House Publishing, Gresham, OR, ©1995. Used by permission of the author.

## MARRIAGE

"18 Attributes to Look for in a Marriage Partner" by Al and Alice Gray, Redmond, Oregon. Used by permission of the authors.

"What Keeps a Marriage Strong?" by Dr. Steve Stephens, Clackamas, Oregon. Used by permission of the author.

"His Needs, Her Needs" by Willard Harley from *His Needs, Her Needs: Basic Needs in Marriage.* Used by permission of Baker Book House, Grand Rapids, Michigan, ©1986.

"Springboards to Deeper Conversation" by Carole Mayhall from *Lord, Teach Me Wisdom.* Used by permission of NavPress, Colorado Springs, CO, ©1979.

"Things *Not* to Say to Your Spouse" by Dr. Steve Stephens from *Marriage: Experience the Best*, published by Vision House Publishers, Gresham, OR, ©1996. Used by permission of the author.

"Things to Say to Your Spouse" by Dr. Steve Stephens from *Marriage: Experience the Best*, published by Vision House Publishers, Gresham, OR, ©1996. Used by permission of the author.

"How to Make Your Marriage Healthy" by Jeff Herring. Reprinted with permission of Knight-Ridder/Tribune Information Services. Condensed from *The Oregonian* newspaper, April 13, 1998.

"20 Ways to Make Your Wife Feel Special" by Al Gray, Redmond, Oregon. Used by permission of the author.

"20 Ways to Make Your Husband Feel Special" by Alice Gray, Redmond, Oregon. Used by permission of the author.

"Togetherness" by Dr. Steve Stephens, Clackamas, Oregon. Used by permission of the author.

"50 Gifts for Marriage" taken from *Understanding the One You Love* by Dr. Steve Stephens, © 1998, published by Harvest House Publishers, Eugene, Oregon 97402. Used by permission.

"Being a Real Man" by Dr. Robert Lewis. Dr. Robert Lewis, teaching pastor at Fellowship Bible Church in Little Rock, Arkansas, also gives leadership to Men's Fraternity, which reaches and teaches men throughout the church and community in the biblical principles of authentic manhood. This exciting ministry is catching on across the country and around the world, where countless small groups are undertaking this study together in churches, neighborhoods, cell blocks, corporate offices, and college campuses. Used by permission.

"Bonds of Intimacy" by Ed Wheat, M.D., condensed from *Love Life for Every Married Couple* by Ed Wheat with Gloria Oakes Perkins. © 1980, 1987 by Ed Wheat, M.D. Used by permission of Zondervan Publishing House.

"Reigniting Romance after Age 50" by Claudia and David Arp from *New Man* magazine, May 1998. Used by permission of Strang Communications.

"20 Creative, Romantic Ideas That Cost under $20" by Gary Smalley with John Trent from *Love is a Decision*, Gary Smalley with John Trent, ©1989, Word Publishing, Nashville, Tennessee. All rights reserved.

"10 Suggestions for Touching" by Ed Wheat, M.D., condensed from a list of twenty-five suggestions from *Love Life for Every Married Couple* by Ed Wheat with Gloria Oakes Perkins. © 1980, 1987 by Ed Wheat, M.D. Used by permission of Zondervan Publishing House.

"Wedding Anniversary Gifts," selected.

## HOME

"Overcoming Clutter" by Allison Allison, an interior designer and homeschooler who resides in Milwaukie, Oregon, with her husband and two children.

"Hints for Kitchen Organization" by Emilie Barnes. Taken from *More Hours in My Day* by Emilie Barnes. © 1982, 1989, 1994 by Harvest House Publishers, Eugene, Oregon 97402. Used by permission.

"How Long to Keep It" excerpted from *Your Financial Organizer*, © 1997 TIAA-CREF. Used by permission.

"Time Makers" by Allison Allison, an interior designer and homeschooler who resides in Milwaukie, Oregon, with her husband and two children.

"Babysitter Checklist" compiled by Alice Gray, Redmond, Oregon. Used by permission of the author.

"Four Axioms of Spending" by Howard L. Dayton, Jr., © 1979 from *Getting Out of Debt*. Used by permission of Tyndale House, Publishers, Inc., Wheaton, IL. All rights reserved. Adapted from *Money, Frustration or Freedom*.

"Simple Ways to Cut Expenses" from *Say Goodbye to Regret* by Robert Jeffress. Published by Multnomah Publishers, Inc., Sisters, OR, © 1998. Used by permission.

"Planning Ahead for Holiday Shopping" by Becky McClure, Milwaukie, Oregon. Used by permission of the author.

"Holiday Entertaining With Less Stress" by Becky McClure, Milwaukie, Oregon. Used by permission of the author.

"Make Your Old Home Feel Like New" by Nancy Larson, Gresham, Oregon. Used by permission of the author.

"Home Safety Tips" by Tom Philbin, Centerport, New York, from *Parade* magazine, February 15, 1998. Used by permission of the author.

"Crime Stoppers' Checklist" excerpted from *About...Keeping Your Home Safe,* a Life Advice® pamphlet produced by MetLife's Consumer Education Center (© 1996 by the Metropolitan Life Insurance Company, New York, NY). Used by permission. All rights reserved. To order a free copy of this booklet or any of the over eighty *Life Advice*® pamphlets, call 1-800-METLIFE or visit their web site at *www.metlife.com*.

"Fire Safety Checklist" excerpted from *About...Keeping Your Home Safe,* a Life Advice® pamphlet produced by MetLife's Consumer Education Center (© 1996 by the Metropolitan Life Insurance Company, New York, NY). See above details.

"Prepare for Disasters" provided by The American Red Cross, Oregon Trail Chapter. Used by permission.

## HEALTH

"Danger Signals of Stress" by Carol Clifton, Ph.D., Licensed Psychologist. Used by permission of the author.

"21 Factors for a Long, Healthy Life" from *The Prevention Index* (Emmaus, PA, Rodale Press). Used by permission.

"Do You Need More Sleep?" by Patricia Anstett. Reprinted with permission of Knight-Ridder/Tribune Information Services.

"Keys to a Lifetime of Fitness" excerpted from *About...Fitness and Exercise,* a Life Advice® pamphlet produced by MetLife's Consumer Education Center (© 1996 by the Metropolitan Life Insurance Company, New York, NY). Used by permission. All rights reserved. To order a free copy of this booklet or any of the over eighty *Life Advice*® pamphlets, call 1-800-METLIFE or visit their web site at *www.metlife.com*.

"Benefits of Exercise" excerpted from *About...Fitness and Exercise,* a Life Advice® pamphlet produced by MetLife's Consumer Education Center (© 1996 by the Metropolitan Life Insurance Company, New York, NY). Used by permission. All rights reserved. See above details.

"10 Simple Ways to Build Exercise into Your Day" by Carl Dreizler and Mary E. Ehemann from 52 Ways to Lose Weight. Used by permission of Thomas Nelson, Inc., Nashville, TN, ©1992.

"Back Savers" from The Back Almanac. Used by permission of Lanier Publishing International, Ltd., Petaluma, California.

"12 Reasons to Keep Your Child Home from School" by Pat Van Diest, R.N. Used by permission of the author.

"10 Ways to Help Prevent Heart Disease" by Terry Shintani and Janice M. T. Miller from 52 Ways to Prevent Heart Disease. Used by permission of Thomas Nelson, Inc., Nashville, TN, ©1993.

"Recognize a Heart Attack!" is taken from the American Heart Association booklet titled Heart Attack and Stroke: Signals and Action. Used by permission.

"Recognize a Stroke!" is taken from the American Heart Association booklet titled Heart Attack and Stroke: Signals and Action. Used by permission.

"Fourteen Warning Signs for Cancer" from the American Cancer Society, Bend, Oregon office. Used by permission. For more information, call 1-800-227-2345.

## CONTENTMENT

"A Better Life" from Taking the Lead by Ron Jenson. Published by Multnomah Publishers, Inc., Sisters, OR, © 1998. Used by permission.

"Choices" from The Seven Laws of the Harvest by John Lawrence. ©1975 published by Kregel Publications, Grand Rapids, MI. Used by permission.

"Nine Essentials for Contented Living" by Goethe.

"A Prayer of Mother Teresa" from Mother Teresa: A Simple Path, compiled by Lucinda Vardey. © 1995 by Mother Teresa. Reprinted by permission of Ballantine Books, a Division of Random House, Inc.

"Leave It to God" from The Finishing Touch, Charles R. Swindoll, ©1994, Word Publishing, Nashville, Tennessee. All rights reserved.

"13 Rules to Live By" by General Colin Powell from Parade magazine, an August 13, 1989 article by David Wallechinsky. Used by permission.

"Day by Day" by Carl Dreizler and Mary E. Ehemann from 52 Ways to Lose Weight. Used by permission of Thomas Nelson, Inc., Nashville, TN, ©1992.

"How Attitude Affects Us" taken from Motivation to Last a Lifetime by Ted W. Engstrom with Robert C. Larson. © 1984 by The Zondervan Corporation. Used by permission of Zondervan Publishing House.

"How to Forfeit Peace" by Elisabeth Elliot from Keep a Quiet Heart. Published by Servant Publications, Ann Arbor, MI, ©1995. Published in the United Kingdom, 1997 edition, by Patersnoster Press, P.O.Box 300, Carisle, Cumbria, CA3 OQS. Used by permission of the author.

"How to Find Peace" by Elisabeth Elliott from Keep a Quiet Heart. Published by Servant Publications, Ann Arbor, MI, ©1995. Published in the United Kingdom, 1997 edition, by Patersnoster Press, P.O.Box 300, Carisle, Cumbria, CA3 OQS. Used by permission of the author.

"12 Reasons to Pray" by John Van Diest. Used by permission of the author.

"12 Things to Pray For" by J. Carl Laney, Professor of Biblical Literature, Western Seminary. Used by permission of the author.

"I'm Thankful For..." by Tami Stephens, Clackamas, Oregon. Used by permission of the author.

"What We Can Control" by John Lawrence from *The Seven Laws of the Harvest*. ©1975. Published by Kregel Publications, Grand Rapids, MI. Used by permission.

"You're Blessed When..." by Eugene H. Peterson from *The Message*. © 1993, 1994, 1995. Used by permission of NavPress Publishing Group, Colorado Springs, CO.

## STANDING STRONG

"Winning Over Worry" by Linda Shepherd from *Love's Little Recipes for Life*. Published by Multnomah Publishers, Inc., Sisters, OR, ©1997. Used by permission.

"In the Eye of the Storm" by Max Lucado from *In the Eye of the Storm*, Max Lucado, © 1991, Word Publishing, Nashville, Tennessee. All rights reserved.

"Overcoming Depression & Discouragement" by Dr. Steve Stephens, Clackamas, Oregon. Used by permission of the author.

"A Positive Focus," Philippians 4:8, *The Holy Bible*, New International Version (NIV), ©1973, 1978, 1984 by International Bible Society, used by permission of Zondervan Publishing House. All rights reserved.

"Stress Busters" by Pam Vredevelt, Licensed Professional Counselor. ©1999. Used by permission of the author.

"Are You Doing Too Much?" by Ramona Richards from *HomeLife* magazine, April 1998. Ramona is a singer, writer, and speaker. Her specialty topics include prayer, single parents, the Internet, and women in the Bible. Contact her ministry at *Psalm98Min@aol.com* or P.O. Box 716, Goodlettsville, TN 37070 for more information. Used by permission.

"Eight Questions to Ask before Saying Yes" by Alice Gray and Dr. Steve Stephens. Used by permission of the authors.

"Nine Goals for Authentic Growth" by Joe D. Batten from *New Man* magazine, March/April 1998. Used by permission of Strang Communications.

"10 Beliefs that Lead to Anger" by Glenda Hotton, MA, COC, LMFT, family counselor in private practice in Valencia, California, specializing in chemical dependency, crisis, and trauma. ©1998. Used by permission.

"Dealing With Anger" by Dr. Steve Stephens from *Marriage: Experience the Best*, published by Vision House Publishing, Gresham, OR, ©1996. Used by permission of the author.

"The World Needs People..." taken from *Motivation to Last a Lifetime* by Ted W. Engstrom with Robert C. Larson. © 1984 by The Zondervan Corporation. Used by permission of Zondervan Publishing House.

## FAMILY FUN

"Top 10 Free Toys for Children" by Crystal Kirgiss, mother of three boys and columnist for the *Detroit Lake Tribune*. ©1996. Used by permission of the author.

"Family Guidelines for Television" by Alice Gray, Dr. Steve Stephens, and John Van Diest. Used by permission of the authors.

"Family Guidelines for Using the Internet," from *New Man* magazine, September/October 1995. Used by permission of Strang Communications.

"The Eight Best Surprises a Kid Ever Had" condensed from a list of ten from *Family Times: Growing Together in Fun and Faith* by Jerry and Patti MacGregor. © 1999 by Harvest House Publishers, Eugene, Oregon 97402. Used by permission.

"20 Fun Activities" by Tami Stephens, Clackamas, Oregon. Used by permission of the author.

"48 Great Books to Read Aloud" by Janice E. Byram, teacher. Used by permission of the author.

"How to Choose a Video for Your Family" by Ted Baehr condensed from *The War Cry*, The Salvation Army magazine, September 10, 1994. Used by permission.

"20 Great Children's Movies" selected from *Family Video Guide to Recommended Movies* edited by John H. Evans. Published by Movie Morality Ministries, Inc., Richardson, TX, © 1996. To order the video guide or to subscribe to a semi-monthly guide called *Preview Family Movie and TV Review*, call 1-800-807-8071 or visit their web site at *www.previewonline.org*.

"20 Great Family Movies" selected from *Family Video Guide to Recommended Movies* edited by John H. Evans. Published by Movie Morality Ministries, Inc., Richardson, TX, © 1996. See above for additional information.

"20 Great Table Games" by Tami Stephens, Clackamas, Oregon. Used by permission of the author.

## FAMILY LIFE

"The Job of Parents" from *Parenting Isn't for Cowards*, James C. Dobson, © 1987, Word Publishing, Nashville, Tennessee. All rights reserved.

"10 Family Commitments" by Dr. Greg Cynaumon from *How to Avoid Alienating Your Kids in 10 Easy Steps*, published by Mood Press, Chicago, IL, © 1993. Used by permission of the author.

"Six Steps to Successful Communication" as cited in *More of...The Best of Bits & Pieces*, Rob Gilbert, Ph.D., editor. © 1997 by The Economics Press, Inc.

"20 Conversation Starters" from *Family Times: Growing Together in Fun and Faith* by Jerry and Patti MacGregor. © 1999 by Harvest House Publishers, Eugene, Oregon 97402. Used by permission.

"Why Divorce Hurts Children" by Archibald Hart from *Moody* magazine, May 1985. Used by permission of the author.

"10 Ways to Be a Great Dad" condensed from the pamphlet *10 Ways to Be A Better Date*, published by The National Fatherhood Initiative. Used by permission.

"Help for Discouraged Parents" from *Parenting Isn't for Cowards*, Dr. James C. Dobson, © 1987, Word Publishing, Nashville, Tennessee. All rights reserved.

"Family Team Building" by Tricia Goyer and Cindy McCormick Martinusen from *HomeLife* magazine, July 1998. Used by permission of Cindy McCormick Martinusen.

"Be a Parent Teachers Like to See" by Joe Neff condensed from *Focus on the Family* magazine, September 1998. Used by permission of the author.

"Five Musts for Every Family" by Gary Chapman from *Five Signs of a Functional Family*, © 1997 by Northfield Publishing, Chicago, Illinois. Used by permission.

## FAMILY VALUES

"Qualities to Pass on to Your Children" taken from *Growing Strong in the Seasons of Life* by Charles R. Swindoll. © 1983 by Charles R. Swindoll, Inc. Used by permission of Zondervan Publishing House.

"The 10 Commandments of Discipline" by Dr. Greg Cynaumon from *How to Avoid Alienating Your Kids in 10 Easy Steps*, © 1993. Used by permission of the author.

"The Six A's of Parenting" by Dr. Steve Stephens, Clackamas, Oregon. Used by permission of the author.

"Parenting 101" by John Rosemond from *Bottom Line Personal*, Vol. 13, No. 3. Family psychologist John Rosemond is the author of eight bestselling parenting books and is one of America's most popular public speakers. For more information, see his web site at *www.rosemond.com*. Used by permission.

"10 Things to Do When Children Are Afraid" by Dr. Steve Stephens, Clackamas, Oregon. Used by permission of the author.

"Jobs Kids Can Do" by Doreen Button, mom to three busy home-school kids. Used by permission of the author.

"Winning Over the Picky Eater" excerpted with permission from *How to Get Your Kid to Eat...But Not Too Much,* Bull Publishing, Palo Alto, CA. For more information about Ellyn Satter's books and teaching materials, see *www.ellynsatter.com* or call 1-800-808-7976.

"Table Manners" by June Hines Moore, etiquette consultant with fifteen years' experience. Author of *You Can Raise a Well-Mannered Child* and *The Etiquette Advantage.*

"When to Teach Your Child Manners" from *You Can Raise a Well-Mannered Child* by June Hines Moore. Used by permission of the author and Broadman & Holman Publishers, 127 Ninth Avenue, North, Nashville, TN 37234, ©1996.

"The 10 Most Important Manners to Teach Your Children" from *You Can Raise a Well-Mannered Child* by June Hines Moore.

## FAMILY LOVE

"Loving Your Kids" by Billy Graham from *God's Little Instruction Book for Dad*, Published by Honor Books, Tulsa, OK, ©1995.

"Today's Kids Desperately Need Heroes Who..." by Marty Wilkins, Milwaukie, Oregon. Used by permission of the author.

"Blessed Are Parents Who..." from The Association for Children and Adults with Learning Disabilities, Pittsburgh, PA. Used by permission.

"A Child's 10 Commandments to Parents" taken from *Getting the Best Out of Your Kids* (a revised and updated edition of the book formerly titled *Parenthood Without Hassles*) by Dr. Kevin Leman. © 1992 by Harvest House Publishers, Eugene, Oregon 97402. Used by permission.

"Meaningful Touch" by Lorri Cardwell-Casey from *HomeLife* magazine. Used by permission of the author. Lorri Cardwell-Casey has over 350 magazine credits. She lives in Bella Vista, AK and can be reached at *lorricasey@aol.com*. Her telephone number is 501-855-0590.

"50 Ways to Love Your Children" by Dr. Steve Stephens from *Stories for the Family's Heart* by Alice Gray. Published by Multnomah Publishers, Inc., Sisters, OR, ©1998. Used by permission of Dr. Steve

Stephens.

"Words for Your Family" from *Leaving the Light On* by Gary Smalley and John Trent. Published by Multnomah Publishers, Inc., Sisters, OR, © 1991. Used by permission.

"10 Ideas for Making a Memorable Mother's Day" by Marilyn McAuley, Milwaukie, Oregon. Used by permission of the author.

"10 Ideas for a Fabulous, Unforgettable Father's Day" by Daniel L. McAuley, Milwaukie, Oregon. Used by permission of the author.

"What Kids Appreciate" by Gary Smalley and John Trent condensed from a list of one hundred from *The Blessing* by Gary Smalley and John Trent. Used by permission of Thomas Nelson, Inc., Nashville, TN, ©1986.

"Long-Distance Grandparenting" by Irene Endicott condensed from *Grandparenting by Grace.* © 1994, Broadman & Holman, 127 Ninth Avenue, North, Nashville, TN 37234. Used by permission.

"Take the Time" reprinted with permission from *Take the Time*, Search Institute, Minneapolis, MN. All rights reserved by Search Institute, 1-800-888-7828. © 1998.

## WISDOM

"Wise Things Your Grandma Told You" by Patti MacGregor from *Family Times: Growing Together in Fun and Faith* by Jerry and Patti MacGregor. © 1999 by Harvest House Publishers, Eugene, Oregon 97402. Used by permission.

"A Short Course in Human Relations" as cited in *More of…The Best of Bits & Pieces,* Rob Gilbert, Ph.D., editor. © 1997 by The Economics Press, Inc.

"Responsibility" by Thomas Jefferson.

"Wise Sayings From the Book of Proverbs" taken from *Come Before Winter* by Charles R. Swindoll. © 1985, by The Zondervan Corporation. Used by permission of Zondervan Publishing House.

"Wise Sayings From Poor Richard's Almanac" by Benjamin Franklin selected from *Poor Richard's Almanac.*

"When Something Right Can Go Wrong" by A. W. Tozer from *The Quotable Tozer,* compiled by Harry Verploegh, Christian Publications, Camp Hill, PA, ©1994. Page 158.

"Seven Things God Hates" from the *NIV Study Bible, New International Version,* ©1985 by the Zondervan Corporation, Grand Rapids, MI.

"Knowing Yourself" by A. W. Tozer from *The Quotable Tozer,* compiled by Harry Verploegh, Christian Publications, Camp Hill, PA, ©1994. Page 165.

"Six Destructive Mistakes" Marcus Tullius Cicero (106-43 B.C.).

"Love…" by St. Paul the Apostle, adapted from 1 Corinthians 13:4–8.

# Coming January 1, 2001!
# Lists To Live By II:
## For Everything That Really Matters

Two hundred lists with power, wisdom, inspiration, and practical advice. Some will move you to action. And some will change your life. These are not books with trivial information. The lists telescope areas of our lives where we have the deepest concerns. The thoughts are succinct, but flow with inspiration and wisdom. Topics include success, friendship, virtue, marriage, home, health, contentment, love, family, faith, and wisdom.

## Stories compiled by authors:

**Alice Gray**, an inspirational conference speaker, leader in women's ministries, creator and compiler of the bestselling Stories for the Heart series.

**Steve Stephens**, licensed psychologist, marriage and family therapist, Ph.D. from Western Seminary, successful seminar speaker. Author of *Marriage: Experience the Best* (Vision House Publishing, 1995), *Understanding the One You Love* (Harvest House, 1998), *Book of Beginnings* (Barbour Books, 1998), Book of Leaders (Barbour Books,1999), *Book of Kingdoms* (Barbour Books, 1999).

**John Van Diest**, founder and publisher of Multnomah Press for twenty years, associate publisher of Multnomah Publishers, graduate of Lewis and Clark college and Dallas Theological Seminary. Serves on various boards including Walk Thru the Bible Ministries. He has traveled around the world to places including Hong Kong, Africa, and Moscow as a speaker and leader for Christian Literature. Creator and compiler of Unsolved Miracles (Multnomah Publishers, 1997), general editor of *10 Reasons Why Jesus Is Coming Again Soon* (Multnomah Publishers, 1998), *10 Answers to Life's Most Perplexing Problems* (Multnomah Publishers, 1998), and *10 Things Satan Doesn't Want You to Know* (Multnomah Publishers, 1998).